Why Do Scenario Planning Extreme?

When it comes to preparing for the future, we are hindered by what we don't know, and by what we think we know. Our values, beliefs and convictions make us see things that aren't there, like "the emperor s new clothes", and make us blind to things that are too threatening to our world views. We need to deal with both if we want to prevail.

Scenario Planning Extreme challenges what we think we know and helps us recognize what we don't. In ten steps it enables open-minded teams to think through several unlikely but possible scenarios and opens their eyes to opportunities for breakthrough success strategies.

"Never has there been a time when identifying the flaws in our thinking processes has been more critical. The fate of the world and our future destiny depend on it. This book demonstrates in a highly readable and understandable way how to do that."

Linda O'Riordan
Director Center for Corporate Social Responsibility
FOM University of Applied Science, Essen

Martin Gillo's insights reflect his professional life in Europe and the US: University-based leadership researcher, Management Consultant. Human Resource Executive in Silicon Valley, Geneva, and Dresden. Managing Director. Politician in Saxony. Saxony's State Minister of Economic Affairs and Labor. For over 15 years Lecturer for Scenario Planning at several universities.

Scenario Planning Extreme

Scenario Planning Extreme

If You Aren't Going Too Far, You're Not Going Far Enough

Martin Gillo

www.scenarioplanningextreme.com

Publisher: BoD · Books on Demand GmbH,
Überseering 33, 22297 Hamburg,
bod@bod.de
Print: Libri Plureos GmbH,
Friedensallee 273, 22763 Hamburg
ISBN: 978-3-7597-2323-9

Dedication

For all those on whose shoulders we stand.

Table of Contents

Glossary of Key Terms   1

Foreword by Charles Hampden-Turner   5

Welcome to Scenario Planning Extreme   9

Part I: Words Teach. Examples Convince   13

1.1 We World Explainers   15

Invented reality   16

Seductive past success: AT&T, IBM, Nokia   19

We fortune tellers   23

Wake up, automotive industry!   28

1.2 This is Scenario Planning Extreme   29

Flying with one foot on the ground:
The Scenario Method/Technique   31

Black Swans. Big changes
            possible overnight   33

Scenario planning extreme defined   34

Extreme times - extreme change   37

1.3 Scenario Planning Extreme – is the CEO's
  Prime Accountability   39

HuLiO reality tunnels   41

When proven paradigms
  are displaced   42

Secret ingredient: co-ownership   44

Extreme scenario planning:
A journey in ten steps   45

How to involve decision-makers   46

1.4 Scenario Planning Extreme in Politics   49

Non-profit NGOs   52

1.5 The Learning Organization   55

Systems thinking   57

Personal mastery   57

Mental models   59

Shared Vision   61

Team learning   62

How do we create a learning organization?   64

1.6 The Power of Multiple Reality Tunnels   69

Group Dynamics, Flow and
  FlowTeam Dynamics   69

Part II: Scenario Planning Extreme for Everyone   75

Step 1: The Team   77

The rules of the seminar   78

Be open for new insights 81

Step 2: The Client 83

Why values are important 85

The external seminar 87

The in-house seminar 88

The pilot project 88

Always two clients in politics 89

Step 3: The Key Question 91

Step 4: Relevant Trends 95

Preparation for the seminar 97

During the seminar 97

From individual observations to the
common trend wall 99

Co-ownership vs. time restrictions 102

Step 5: From Trends to Extreme Scenarios 103

Step 6: Storyboards 109

Scenarios as personas 116

Step 7: Strategies 119

Transform or adapt! 120

Strategies with rear-view mirror perspective 124

Three scenario-specific strategies 127

Step 8: Scenario Alert Signals 129

Identifying supporters of our strategies 131

Step 9: Winning over the Client 135

The external seminar 136

Winning over the internal client 138

Co-creating scenarios 139

Step 10: Implementing Scenario Planning Extreme 145

Part III: Coping With an Extreme World 155

3.1 Career Planning with Extreme Scenarios 159

Careers in any future 161

Start by doing something 164

Three prototype scenario careers 165

Do something 166

Meaningful scenario careers at any age 168

3.2 Extreme Scenarios of Migration and Integration 171

A long-term perspective for successful
integration in Europe 172

The situation in 2015 173

Thinking about long-term solutions 173

Four scenarios 174

Strategies to strengthen European
integration and identity 175

Summary 178

Is political reflection without blinkers
too dangerous? 179

3.3 Alternatives to Drug Bans 183

The courage to think about extremes 185

What would be better than a ban on drugs? 190

Thinking Beyond Taboos   191

    Fearless reflection on other controversial topics 192

3.4 Succeed Together in Every Future   195

Attachments   203

Selected Literature   207

Acknowledgements   211

Index   213

References Used plus
some Personal Notes   219

Glossary of Key Terms

*1*926ing: The human tendency not to give up a deep conviction even in the face of contrary evidence, but to hold on to it with even greater conviction.

Assimilation-contrast effect: Information that is perceived as close to one's own opinion is seen as confirmation of it. Information that is too far removed from one's own convictions is emotionally rejected.

Black swans: The sudden occurrence of unforeseen changes that were previously thought impossible; named for the surprising discovery in Australia that the swans there were not white, but black.

Co-ownership: People identify themselves as co-owners of an idea if they contributed meaningfully to its development. Co-ownership is one of the strongest forces of human motivation.

Design thinking: thinking like a product developer. It is about understanding, observing, defining a point of view, finding ideas, creating a prototype, testing it, improving it, and repeating this process step by step until the solution is found.

Human Like Organization (HuLiO): It can be helpful to view an organization as analogous to a human being, possessing its own sense of meaning and purpose, striving to reach its full potential, and aspiring to achieve enduring longevity. This applies to companies, HuLiO(c), political organizations, HuLiO(p) and non-governmental organizations HuLiO(n).

Imaginate: To create a clear and vivid mental image of a specific abstract concept by seeing or imagining what others cannot yet perceive. Applied to a scenario, the vivid mental image would include a story of how it came about and what it looks like that is clear enough that one could author a story or make a movie about it.

Intersubjectivity: When people with different perspectives agree on what is real. It shows whether what we perceive to be true may likely to be true.

Learning Organization: An organization which recognizes that its most important competitive advantage lies in continuous learning, and which acts accordingly. A Learning Organization continuously evolves by encouraging and enabling its members to acquire, share, and apply knowledge. It fosters a culture of innovation, adaptability, and collaboration,

allowing it to respond effectively to changes in the environment.

Meaning of life: my self-image, which is derived from my past, my affections and loyalties; from human history as it has been handed down to me; from my talents as well as my insights and knowledge; from the things I believe in; from the things and people I love; from the values for which I am prepared to make sacrifices.

Positive deviation: In every community, there are people whose unconventional behavior has led to solutions to seemingly unsolvable problems. It is important to discover these and win them over for the benefit of the community.

Quantitative blinkers: The danger of self-imposed blindness to the potential for extreme developments in the future by tying the range of one's analyses to calculated extrapolations of the past. By focusing narrowly on numerical or measurable data and neglecting qualitative, contextual, or subjective factors, one risks ignoring the possibility of extremes. Those who fail to prepare to deal with such extremes are left vulnerable to significant failures should they arise.

Reality: The landscape of the world as it is. Unfortunately, it is only indirectly recognizable to us.

Reality tunnel: What we perceive all around us is not the objective or "real" world, only our own individual reality tunnel, which reflects a construct shaped by our self-created mental maps. These maps show our personal interpretation or "take" on the world, based on how we see or believe we see it. Crucially, the reality tunnel excludes aspects of the real world that we may unconsciously or deliberately ignore. While we can never completely escape our individual reality tunnels, we can work on improving our self-constructed mental maps, by refining and expanding them to better align with the contextual complexities of the actual world.

Rear-view mirror perspective: The opportunities of innovative strategies are easier to recognize and develop if you look back from the future to the present.

Scenario Alert Signals: Subtle indications that a particular scenario is on the verge of becoming reality, signaling the need to activate and implement the strategies prepared in anticipation.

Shock doctrine: Naomi Klein's controversial thesis that the global free market has not triumphed through democratic means and that unchecked capitalism does not automatically lead to democracy. She argues that over the last 70 years, Western politics has repeatedly relied on violence and orchestrated shocks to impose its perspectives on the world.

Siamese Twins: Our reality tunnels are inextricably linked to our purpose in life. If you change your reality tunnel, you also change your purpose in life and vice versa.

Stakeholders: Interest groups, persons, corporations, or institutions that are directly or indirectly affected by the activities of an organization and attempt to influence it in return.

Storyboard: The concrete visualization of an evolving story, movie, or scenario with its details. In Scenario Planning Extreme, it is used to visualize scenarios with their most important trends and their development from the current situation 25 years into the future.

Time caravan of consent: Temporal sequence of social and organizational changes. The trendsetters lead the way, followed later by the early adopters and later again by most trend followers. Perennial skeptics bring up the rear with a long delay.

Unfreeze – change – refreeze: The process by which groups open themselves up to consider change, identify new behaviors that better reflect their needs and interests, and integrate these behaviors as a permanent part of their future conduct. This approach is widely recognized as the most effective method to create lasting social change and is equally applicable to drive transformation within organizations.

Foreword by
Charles Hampden-Turner

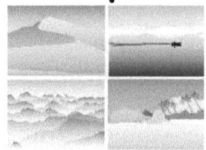

*P*lanning has a rather checkered history and a blemished reputation. A planned economy is identified with politicians "seizing the commanding heights of an economy," and imposing socialism. Autocratic governments that demand people obey also expect events to be controllable by them. They are especially hostile to market turbulence. One thousand tractors rust in the field because a bureaucrat forgot to order a No. 7 lug-head bolt. Had its price been allowed to rise the bolts would have manifested themselves. The Soviet Union and Warsaw Pact countries were all planned economies, and we all saw what happened to them once the Wall came down.

Over the next fifteen years virtually every department of Long-rage Planning in the US closed. When one or two global corporations dominated in the style of IBM, then it was possible to plan, and the future was doing more of what you had done in the past. But when there is a dozen or more competitors and East Asia is on the march, then straight-line trajectories of different companies collide with unforeseeable impacts. We have moved into a VUCA world. The letters stand for Volatile, Uncertain, Complex and Ambiguous. To forecast is to steam full ahead though an ocean of icebergs. You will collide and sink. Those who plan often mistake their expectations and their iron fists for what is actually happening. Autocrats are especially prone to error.

It looked very much as if we had to give up on planning all together. Those extolling markets counselled that we stand like Venus's flytraps, snapping shut at any insect that approached. All you could really do was react. Short-termism was the order of the day. Markets were like bumper cars, with bangs and shouts. Luckily, there were at least two major institutions who felt they could not give up on planning long-term. The US defense department and its consulting partner the Hudson Institute were spending and collecting billions of dollars and Royal Dutch Shell faced a Middle East that was a tinder box of animosities. Great powers tried to assure their oil supplies by arming proxies to the hilt. What would happen next baffled everyone and Israel, a European enclave, was the potential detonator.

Yet in any conflict there will be winners, losers, those who persist—and very occasionally a negotiated settlement. It is possible to imagine three to four such outcomes and make ready for any of them to occur. It follows that another approach to planning is to make ready for all four contingencies, with a scenario for each of them as events develop. You then rely on the scenario that is more nearly coming true. Two years before this writer joined Group Planning at Shell, it had warned that OPEC might form a form a cartel and raise prices. Shell was prepared for this and gained considerably from this intelligence. Three years later group planning employed more than sixty people and two Harvard Business School professors and every Operating Organization prepared national scenarios to fit within the global ones they had been given.

It is important to realize that neither Shell nor the Pentagon gambles on which scenario will come true. You do not bet on your organization or nation. The point is to prosper whichever scenario comes true and be ready for each and all. Even if a scenario is "bad," being ready for it gives you a distinct advantage, like a ship that battens its hatches before a storm. Shell had a department for strategy, but these were now road tested against different scenarios and were expected to find advantages in each one. Every scenario was a narrative, an imagined end-state, with a story about how we got there from here. A current argument can have different outcomes or alternative futures.

One of the major characteristics of scenarios is that for the most part they are wrong. At best only one in three or four scenarios will come true and even that, true only in part. It seems to a lot of trouble to take over, being mostly wrong. Except that being wrong is an important part of learning, perhaps the main part. What we notice in life are differences between what we expected and what came about. When we are correct, we are at first satisfied, even complacent, but thereafter cease to notice. If you wrap someone up in a warm cocoon, which has the same temperature as the person's blood, then differences disappear and within a remarkably short time, a matter of hours, intelligence deteriorates sharply followed by consciousness. We are aware of where our skin stops, and our environment starts and when that borderline is obscured, mental processes deteriorate severely.

If you are watching the news on TV, then it is what you did not expect that registers. You must make hundreds of guesses in order to stay alert and what you notice are the discrepancies. When we commit an embarrassing faux pas, we remember for days! Being wrong most of the time is essential to keep asking questions, which is why skepticism plays such a key role in science. You assume you are wrong as the path to verification. When we researched those in Shell who had worked with scenarios, we found that they were much more alert and knowledgeable about current affairs. Whenever do you witness an event, you ask yourself, what longer-term scenario does this apply?

Many of us are familiar with ambiguous pictures, the ascending staircase that curiously then starts to descend. But when asked to draw this most of us could not do it. We have no map or scene in our minds as to how this contradiction operates. We would need to stare long and hard at the original. But scenarios give us this map and when it happens, we can recognize it and know what to do. We can see that which we have mapped in advance. When those born blind have their sight restored, they can at first recognize only what they once touched. We learn how to see. Adults with as much as five years of normal sight cannot "see" or even describe the front of a car. When blind no one let them linger there and they never felt it. Scenarios teach us to see. They are mental models of what is otherwise strange. Puppies or kittens raised in a box of horizontal stripes, cannot "see" a vertical shape for several days and bump into chair legs and table legs. We see what we can encounter.

Scenarios are the secret of resilience, of being bowled over by events yet being ready to pick yourself up and carry on. It is how we rally from setback that matters in the VUCA world. We quake over the Wizard of Oz and his fire breathing image until we spot that elderly man pulling levers. Scenarios de-mystify and see through shock doctrines.

I very much hope you enjoy this book. The author is particularly profound on this topic.

7

Welcome to
Scenario Planning Extreme

The secret of success lies in
being ready when
the opportunity presents itself.
Benjamin Disraeli

Our world is characterized by radical changes[1] including Black Swans[2]. Changes we did not think possible yesterday are shaping our lives today. The industrial history of the last 50 years is full of examples of companies that dominated their market but refused to accept the possibility of exponential change, even when they witnessed it, until they failed.

Scenario Planning Extreme is a surprising answer to the question of how we should plan for the long-term future of 25 years even though we cannot know what it will look like. We "Imaginate" several vastly different futures at the same time and then prepare strategies for each one. Scenario Planning Extreme deliberately focuses on extreme futures that we often ignore for a variety of reasons.

Quantitative methods are useful for short to medium-term planning in times of moderate change. However, even the best mathematical formulas fail when it comes to exponential changes. This also applies to the scenario technique/method known in German-speaking countries, which is significantly tied to quantitative trend analyses.

Our answer to the question of how we can prepare for extreme changes is this book on Scenario Planning Extreme. It shows how we can prepare for exponential change in today's world. It deliberately focuses on imagination and diversity of perspectives that reflect as much as possible the diversity of the world in which organizations must prepare for their future. The approach works with purely intersubjective, qualitative means, meaning it relies on the perceptions of a highly diverse group of individuals, free of quantitative methods that intentionally or unintentionally limit the breadth of future possibilities considered and with which organizations effectively put blinkers on themselves. As we shall see, this can lead to catastrophic consequences. Future possibilities cannot be restricted. The future will be what it will be, whether we like it or not.

In Scenario Planning Extreme, we imagine the space of all possible futures and usually develop four vastly different scenarios as reference points. This is comparable to triangulation used in creating maps. Scenario Planning Extreme can be carried out by all interested, committed, curious and unbiased teams in ten easy-to-understand steps. This approach has proven itself repeatedly in seminars at various universities for many years. The aim of Scenario Planning Extreme is to develop strategies with which the opportunities and threats corresponding to the respective scenarios can be recognized and exploited; because even in threatening times, billions in profits can be made, as George Soros[3] has shown repeatedly.

Scenario Planning Extreme operates within an open-ended world of imagination that is visualized using qualitative examples, analogies and metaphors. These alternate in the book with descriptions of the step-by-step development of future scenarios and the corresponding success strategies.

To describe this with a metaphor: Reading our book is like a ski run of varied activities where the Scenario Planning Extreme approach is our ski run down the slope of a mountain. The challenging mountain we must ski down represents our own reality tunnels, because we can only imagine reality indirectly through the ideas we have constructed of it. Our reality tunnels contain many mental crevices, cliffs and trees that can abruptly end our descent. Instead of barreling down the mountain of our reality tunnels in a straight line, we glide down in many enjoyable S-curves and thus arrive safely in the valley of future opportunities, with new knowledge and a reality tunnel that is closer to reality. We can then utilize these "learning loops" to our advantage.

This makes our book both an instruction manual for Scenario Planning Extreme and a kaleidoscope of examples of human thinking, wishful thinking and action. The first concerns the question: How do you conduct a Scenario Planning Extreme project? The second sheds light on how we can continuously refine our reality tunnels to better approximate reality itself.

Part I describes the conceptual underpinnings of Scenario Planning Extreme and the insights into how we perceive the world.

Part II describes how Scenario Planning Extreme is conducted in ten clear and comprehensible steps. How do you conduct such a project? Our recommendations concern both the planning and execution of Scenario Planning Extreme seminars and the subsequent implementation of the approach in organizations. They reflect experiences in the development, organization, and implementation of change in Germany, Europe, and the US from the perspective of a former consultant and decision-maker in business and politics.

And yet every change is new and different. All innovations have their own opportunities and uncertainties and require users to have the courage to find and follow their own path. This is exactly what we wish for our readers. These times of rapid change help those who are ready for new opportunities, to recognize them early on and seize the chance to make effective use of them.

Part III shows how Scenario Planning Extreme can also help us with our individual life planning. It shows us how we can recognize different career options that are attractive and meaningful to us. We also look at two controversial topics that are de facto political taboos: the long-term potential impact of up to a million immigrants arriving in Europe each year from the Middle East and North Africa, and the impact of our current approach to the "war on drugs" as declared initially by US president Richard Nixon. We show how Scenario Planning Extreme can help explore these difficult topics with intent to find reasonable alternatives to the currently unreasonable solutions ... that do more harm than good. If we continue to willfully ignore these growing problems, we may end up being overwhelmed by them eventually.

In the spirit of lifelong learning, we suggest that interested parties use a "Copy Exact" perspective during their first Scenario Planning Extreme project, and in subsequent projects consider how they can adapt the initial approach ever better to the circumstances and needs of their own organization. Ideally, each project should fit the client and their objectives like a tailor-made suit.

Finally, Scenario Planning Extreme can also help us in our daily lives. There is something very liberating about always keeping your eyes open to emerging changes and at the same time thinking about the different options for dealing with them. In this way, we learn that there is more than one way to deal successfully with almost any situation. People spend a lot of money with therapists to slowly realize this insight.

Our industry case studies are described with interest and empathy. The author would of course be delighted if the companies in focus could contribute their internal views on these case studies, which could be included in a future edition of this book.

This book reflects the author's personal views and his experiences in business and politics. It also describes relevant examples from his life, referring to himself as Martin. This is intended to create an equal relationship between author and reader and engage readers in a shared conversation. When referring to a specific person, we use the term "she," in the same way it has typical for many centuries to use the term "he."

The book presents itself as a mediator of a great idea. It offers practitioners suggestions and encourages them to open themselves up to a wide spectrum of future possibilities. It is more of a fine art than a scientific treatise. Despite over 150 references and personal views, I am happy to leave the scientific anchoring of the topic to future authors.

Scenario Planning Extreme is both simple and difficult at the same time. It is intellectually easy to follow the ten logical steps of its approach. It is emotionally difficult because it also requires us to set aside some of our dearly held beliefs and to take unlikely and even "unacceptable" trends just as seriously as those that confirm our points of view.

Readers who are more comfortable with quantitative methods are invited to embrace the qualitative approach of Scenario Planning Extreme, enjoy the journey, and learn to recognize and appreciate the value of this approach.

Part I
Words Teach. Examples Convince.

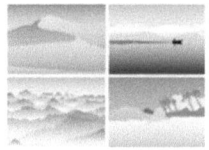

You can only see well with your heart.
Antoine St. Exupéry

...and sometimes badly.
Martin Gillo

The essential is invisible to the eyes.
Antoine St. Exupéry

... until we also see through the eyes of others, ...
including those of our enemies.
Martin Gillo

*W*e are all convinced that we see reality as it is. But we are mistaken, as Plato warned us with his allegory of the cave. East Asian thinkers expressed this even more blatantly with the parable of the blind men and the elephant. In the story, each blind man can only touch a part of the animal, leading them to misunderstand and fail to recognize the elephant in its entirety.

We often only see what we want to see, e.g., causal connections, even if there are none, but they fit well into our world view. This also applies the other way around. We often do not see what we do not want to see.

Why is that so? Welcome to the world of fears and hopes, likes, and dislikes, the loftiest worldviews and the deepest convictions.

This applies to everyone, including each of us and our beliefs, which have become truths for us. Two people with opposing points of view agree on a test to see who is right. And after the test, both are certain that the test result has confirmed their conviction. For us, this logical contradiction is often the rule. We will show many such examples in this book. Every time we put ourselves "in other people's shoes", we may realize that we would have acted similarly in their situation, and we can learn from this.

How can we free ourselves from distortions in our views of reality? Can Scenario Planning Extreme help us to achieve this? Yes! Preferably with the perspectives of the Living and the Learning Organizations. More on that later...

1.1
We World Explainers

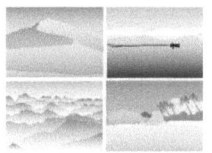

Everything is based on conjecture.
Marcus Aurelius

*S*cenario Planning Extreme is one of the means and methods used to prepare for the future and thus profit from it. Let us look at some of the historical ways and means by which we humans have tried to predict the future throughout our long history, some of which we still use today. From today's perspective, this has led to both amusing misunderstandings and tragic disasters. We describe here the context of all strategic preparations. It is important to understand the uncertainties and misjudgments in any planning.

The desire to explain the world is as old as humanity itself. We want to understand it, rule over and benefit from it and, for some time now, live in harmony with it. This goes hand in hand with the desire to predict the future as successfully as possible, using a wide variety of means and methods.

Humans have always wanted to know where and how best to obtain or produce food, how to optimally use nature including its animals, how to find out where mineral resources can be found and how to utilize them to make their lives easier, how best to make friends with other people or fight against them, how to organize themselves and thus build an empire or how to destroy someone else's. For some time now, we have even been working on understanding our own intelligence to create artificial intelligence and use it to our advantage.

The history of humankind is also the history of predictions ... and very often of failures. Why is that the case?

Invented Reality

With the provocative book title "The Invented Reality", Paul Watzlawick[4] confronted us in the 1980s with our inability to recognize reality itself. What we perceive is not reality itself, but only a reality tunnel made up of mental maps that we have constructed of it and that we can improve during our lives - provided we make an active effort to do so. A generation later, Thomas Metzinger[5] describes this as our "ego tunnel" from which we cannot escape, a very apt term.

In the context of Scenario Planning Extreme, we will use the term "reality tunnel" as originally proposed by Timothy Leary[6], because it emphasizes that it is up to us to constantly re-construct it to closer approximate reality. The walls of our reality tunnels consist of our mental maps of what we think is reality. Reality is the landscape itself. Since we cannot see the landscape, we can only act according to our self-constructed reality tunnels.

We define the concept of reality tunnels via the detour of the definition of the meaning of life, as inspiringly formulated by John W. Gardner:[7]

> *"Meaning is not something you stumble across, like the answer to a riddle or the prize in a treasure hunt. Meaning is something you build into your life. You build it out of your <u>own past</u>, out <u>of your affections</u> and <u>loyalties</u>, out of the <u>experience of humankind</u> as it is passed on to you, out of your <u>own talent</u> and <u>understanding</u>, out of the <u>things you believe in</u>, out of the <u>things</u> and <u>people you love</u>, out of the <u>values for which you are willing to sacrifice</u> something. The ingredients are there. You are the only one who can put them together into that unique pattern that will be your life. Let it be a life that has dignity and meaning to you. If it does, then the particular balance of success or failure is of less account. "[8]* (underlining mine)

Our definition of the reality tunnel follows this literally:

16

We construct our reality tunnels ourselves in our minds from the following elements:

- Our past
    - o Our affections and loyalties
    - o The history of humankind as it has been handed down to us.
- Our competences, preferences, and choices:
    - Our talents, insights, and knowledge.
    - The things we choose to believe in.
    - The things and the people we love.
    - The values for which we are prepared to make sacrifices.

We juxtapose the individual meaning of life and the individual reality tunnel intentionally. For us, they are Siamese Twins. This makes it clear why our constructed maps in our tunnels of reality are always a mixture of facts and ideas, of truth and wishful thinking. Of the ten elements of our definition of the reality tunnel, only three are based on information. If our reality tunnel is confronted with a contradiction, its Siamese Twin, meaning of life, wants to defend itself - and vice versa, as we will see.

Our reality tunnel quickly creates a distorted picture of reality as soon as it

- Calls our loyalties into question.
- Threatens the order and institutions we believe in.
- Makes people we love appear in a bad light.
- Calls the values to which we are committed into question.
- Seems to shake our sense and the very meaning of our life.

For such situations, our reality tunnel has developed numerous defense mechanisms, often invisible to us, which can prevent us from recognizing contradictions between the reality tunnel and reality itself. For example, those who see their working environment threatened by trends find it easy to play them down or even deny them, as we will show.

But reality does not care about our reality tunnels. Reality is what it is. It is up to us to constantly work on adapting our reality tunnels to the constantly changing real reality landscape so that we can be successful in it, no matter how it changes.

Fortunately, there is a wide variety of individual reality tunnels. Even in a conformist society, there will always be people who have the courage to speak out when they think the emperor's new clothes are fictitious. They may not reach those loyal to the emperor, but many others will feel liberated and validated in their own reality tunnels, that differed from the narrative prescribed by the emperor.

Most people are not aware that they only see their own reality tunnels. It takes courage and lifelong learning to become and remain aware of one's imperfect reality tunnel character and to work on getting closer and closer to the constantly changing world through lifelong testing, tuning, and learning. It helps to view your own reality tunnel as a prototype model that can and should be constantly tested through failure and adapted to reality.

Two examples may help to illustrate the difference between reality tunnel and reality, between map and landscape. In the automotive industry, navigation systems were first introduced by luxury brands. Martin recalls a report that a driver drove his BMW into a river in northern Germany at night because his navigation system indicated a bridge over the river. However, it was a ferry. The navigation device did not match the reality. The driver complained to BMW and demanded compensation. A spokesperson for BMW replied something like this: 'We are pleased about the acceptance of our navigation devices, but we also assume that drivers pay attention to the road.' A truck driver in Switzerland had a similar experience in 2010.[9] In both cases, the drivers confused the map with the landscape. This is akin to mistaking the signpost for the destination.

If we want to be and remain successful in life, we should constantly put the mental maps in our reality tunnels to the test by learning in a safe environment and trying to consciously let them fail and then improve them to succeed in the real world. We consider Scenario Planning Extreme to be one of the best tools to achieve this.

It is easy for our reality tunnels to approximate reality when it comes to recurring, repeatable processes. In areas where we have little or no experience, they can quickly become and remain unrealistic. This holds especially true for the prediction of an uncertain future.

Seductive Past Success:
AT&T, IBM, Nokia

Hanging on to past success is one of the worst business world's errors. It makes organizations overestimate the robustness of their success recipes and underestimate the potential impact of change on their world. Even the best quantitative methods for planning the future do not change the principle that the future is unknown and open eventually. It surprises us repeatedly. It cannot be predicted, and yet we keep trying. The history of industrial revolutions is littered with examples of catastrophic misjudgments about the impact of groundbreaking innovations, especially by companies that were previously successful. Below we will look at three companies: IBM, AT&T, and Nokia. Every company is liable to make catastrophic mistakes, even large global corporations like these three. We will learn about some of their strategic failures from Martin's perspective of the US semiconductor industry, i.e., from outside the three companies.

IBM and the PC: IBM[10] was founded in 1911 and is now active in 175 countries with a focus on computers, services, software, supercomputers, and research. The corporation holds over 150,000 patents, six Nobel Prizes and six Turing Prizes[11]. But it, too, occasionally makes catastrophic mistakes, two of which we will take a closer look at now.

When it comes to quantitative planning, no one can second best IBM. For decades, this corporate giant had been the most successful computer manufacturer in the world. Its mainframe computers made the American Apollo moon landing possible. All through the 1980s, its products were a permanent fixture in every major computer center in the Western world.

In the early 1980s, the company decided to develop a new input device for its mainframe computers, which it would call a personal computer (PC). It also calculated optimistic forecasts for the annual sales figures of the designed PC and came up with 280,000 units per year, as it explained to AMD[12] . This figure was too low for her to develop her own microprocessor and operating system for this device. It therefore decided to adopt the Disc Operating System (DOS) from Microsoft, Intel's[13] microprocessor and the associated peripheral chips from AMD, which these two companies were to produce in partnership going forward. IBM also developed a small vault chip to protect the PC from copycats.

Where IBM saw an intelligent input device, the world discovers a personal computer with which anyone can write and/or use many different programs. Many third-party manufacturers design stand-alone programs for the PC. Many customers, including large-scale enterprises and the public discover that the PC liberates them from having to use large computers.

A short time later, a small manufacturer develops a so-called jailbreak chip with which IBM's own vault chip can be bypassed. Overnight, many third-party manufacturers enter the market with lookalike PCs that match the performance of IBM PCs, at around half the price of the original. It would have been high time for IBM to reconsider the potential of the PC in the computer world. But it did not. It too apparently underestimated this with 1926ing. Eventually, the worldwide annuals sales figures for PCs grew not to hundreds of thousands, but to hundreds of millions of devices, although they were no longer produced by IBM.

Intel was the first to recognize the potential of replacing the work of mainframe computers by massively interconnecting many PC cores. In the mid-1980s, Intel and the California Institute of Technology created a supercomputer for scientific applications with 64 Intel 8086/8087 processors. A few years later, Intel succeeded in building the fastest computer in the world, the ASCI Red Computer with thousands of parallel cores. [14].

Here, too, IBM, stuck in 1926ing, refused to take the existential threat to its mainframes seriously. And thus begins the triumphal march of parallel processing computer data centers, in which many thousands of PCs are interconnected with Intel chips and replace IBM-style mainframes. As of 2024, this market was dominated by companies such as Amazon, Cisco, Google, Microsoft, and Oracle.[15]

The story of PC and IBM is the story of the inadequacy of quantitative, forecast-based planning ... and of not wanting to recognize that inadequacy. This raises the question of whether it is the heroes of the status quo who are most likely to ignore the potentially extreme consequences of innovative ideas. Is it because it threatens to end their current position of strength? Imagine the top IBM managers who have made billions for the organization with mainframes and are highly respected. And they are part of the deliberations about how seriously the company should take new signals for PC-based computing. That would be like calling into question the importance of their own careers and those of thousands of their employees. So, 1926ing is humanly understandable - and economically unforgivable.

AT&T, Nokia, and the cell phone: For many decades, the AT&T Corporation[16] was the largest telecommunications group in the world with over one million employees. In 2005, AT&T was acquired by its former subsidiary SBC Communications, which now uses the name AT&T Inc to offer mobile phone services.

Until the 1970s, the AT&T Corporation was extremely successful in the US. De facto every household had their wired telephone connection. And not only that: every store, every petrol station, every train station, every public building, and most streets were equipped with public telephones from AT&T? that anyone can use at any time for a few cents for local calls.

The idea of mobile telephony emerged in the 1980s. What about developing phones for businesspeople who could make calls on the move? AT&T initially decides to go for it, but thinks: why develop an expensive cell phone that is also expensive to operate? Their consultant McKinsey calculates a potential global market for cell phones of 900,000 units[17] per year. This is not enough for the global corporation AT&T, and it exits the up-and-coming cell phone market. Was McKinsey convinced that it could calculate the future? In the long term, it was wrong by a factor of 1000. Was AT&T impressed by the prestige of the world's leading consulting firm? We do not know. Its exit from the burgeoning mobile market marginalized the company and drove it financially against the wall.

Quite different for the Finnish corporation Nokia, a company over 150 years old. Nokia started out with sawmills, rubber products, and electrical cables. In 2023, it operated in one hundred countries, employed 92,000 people, and generated annual sales of twenty-five billion € in 2022. [18]

With the advent of mobile telephony, the Nokia CEO during the 1980s realizes that it is also ideal for her personally, and not just for him: Finland is the land of 10,000 lakes. If you spend the weekend or vacations at "your" lake, you are unreachable by phone. No wonder Nokia commits itself to the developing cell phone market and the associated infrastructure, recognizes this as a fantastic opportunity and puts its heart and resources into it. Other European manufacturers are doing the same and jointly develop a European standard for digital mobile communications, GSM (for Groupe Speciale Mobile), without AT&T's involvement.

What Nokia and its European competitors recognize and what AT&T overlooks is the issue of social status in communication. The one who is called has a higher social status, not the one who calls. Therefore, everyone who is someone wants to be called, no matter where they are.

Why is AT&T sticking to its assessment despite the growing success of the emerging cell phone market? It must be 1926ing. The consequences of this self-inflicted blindness to the potential of cell phones have been disastrous. During his student days in the early 1970s, Martin occasionally dreamed of a career at AT&T because it seemed to him the safest and most interesting of all career options for social psychologists. Later, he was glad that it had remained just a dream.

For Nokia, the decision for cell phones becomes a ride on the tiger. The organization becomes the world's largest manufacturer of cell phones. In 2007, its global market share exceeds 50 %.

Nokia, Apple, and the iPhone: In the same year, Steve Jobs[19] presents the Apple iPhone[20] to the world. You can use it to text, take photos, record videos, listen to music, author emails, and use 100,000 apps. Oh yes, *"and one more thing!"*, you can also make phone calls with it!

Nokia is just as surprised by this as the rest of the world and calculates the future of the smartphone market. It utilizes the best methods of quantitative strategic planning, looks at the past of the cell phone market and concludes that the iPhone is technically inferior to Nokia phones and will therefore remain a niche product. And what Apple's IOS operating system can do, Nokia's own Symbian system should soon be able to do as well[21] ... But it could not.

It would have been easy for Nokia to enter the smartphone market with a suitable operating system. The Android operating system was up for sale. Nokia showed no interest. Google seized the opportunity.

Even as sales of Apple's iPhone and the various Android phones, such as SAMSUNG, grow exponentially, Nokia keeps on 1926ing until it is too late to catch up.

The result? Not the smartphone, but the cell phone has de facto become a niche product. It is mostly for the elderly for whom the smartphone is too complicated. The situation is completely different for Apple and various manufacturers of Android smartphones. Today, two-thirds of the world's population owns such a device.

For us, the case study of Nokia's strategic miscalculation is particularly interesting. It was Nokia that benefited from AT&T's 1926ing, recognizing and harnessing the potential of mobile telephony despite the lack of sufficient data at the time. What might have caused Nokia, as the global market leader, to drastically underestimate the potential of the smartphone through its own 1926ing?

When it comes to important decisions, you want to be as certain as possible. This is a good principle that has proven itself repeatedly when making short-term decisions. No wonder people also want to apply it successfully to questions about the long-term future. The only problem is that it is absurd to calculate the future in the long term. Those who attempt it regardless expose themselves to the risk of making catastrophically flawed decisions. The desire to calculate the future is inherently unattainable. The future cannot be calculated or predicted with accuracy in the long-term.

Why do we repeatedly fall into such traps?

We Fortune Tellers

What does the future look like? Are there laws according to which it will develop? Is it predetermined? And if so, how? If we knew what the future would look like, we could take advantage of and benefit from it. In the course of human history, a variety of beliefs were developed about how the future will unfold. Our ancestors invented them to create order and predictability in an uncertain world, to help themselves prepare for and make the most of it. Some of them are still in use today.

I. The course of the world is an ever-repeating cycle: The success strategy: Accept and adapt. This applies to nature and agriculture. However, people wanted and still wish to believe that such a principle of order exists and can be applied to all other areas of their lives as well. It is no wonder that the astrology belief we humans developed became remarkably successful and still is.

In Chinese astrology, there is an annual sequence of 12 years that repeats itself eternally. Each of the 12 years has its own animal sign with associated characteristics. Each year shapes the personality profile of people depending on their year of birth. When Martin hears about this for the first time, he spontaneously thinks about his first day at school and the other children in first grade with him who have completely distinct characteristics from him. The idea that they should all share his personality type strikes him as absurd. But over a billion people beg to differ. They identify with the animal characteristics attributed to them. Who is right?

Is self-knowledge proof of the truth of astrological statements? As a teaching assistant at a Midwestern university in the US, Martin repeats with the participants a psychological experiment by psychologist Bertrand Forer[22] from the 1920s. As a result, everyone receives a psychological profile evaluated across ten personality factors, with each factor rated on a five-point scale. Remarkably, 90% of the students are amazed by how accurately the profile matches their self-assessment of their own personality. They are even more astonished when they find out that they have all received identical personality profiles.

Our Western astrology had its origins in the Middle East. It works with twelve signs of the zodiac. They are supposed to determine a person's personality depending on the month of birth. Is that more credible? During his time studying at University in the US, Martin is asked by a young woman about his date of birth during an informal conversation. She is a professional astrologer who predicts the future for many of her fellow students. She enjoys such a good reputation that she can charge a fee for her services and make a good living from it. Martin is fascinated by this and spontaneously suggests a little experiment: "*If the stars determine your personality, should it not work the other way round as well? If you knew my personality, wouldn't you also know my sign?* She agrees. '*How about a little experiment? You ask me any question you want, and I will answer you truthfully. My friends are here with me, and they would tell you straight away if I were lying.*"

No sooner said than done. An hour later, she has no more questions, thinks for a while, and names a star sign. Wrong. Another star sign. Wrong again. After six failed attempts, Martin tells her his star sign. And she immediately bursts out: *"I knew it!"*

Pay attention! The test was conducted to show who was right. Martin saw his rejection of astrology confirmed. And the sympathetic astrologer found her belief confirmed. How could she do that? How about: She earned her living with astrology. It is easier to interpret the results to suit your own interests than to lose your livelihood. Let us cut her some slack. We may also act the same way in areas that are dear to us.

Not only in this case: our reality tunnels are resistant to contradictions when they question our meaning and reasoning of life. As soon as it comes to questions and matters of deep convictions or faith, questioning facts comes to nothing and tends to fall into emptiness.

II. The course of the world has an ultimate destination: In this belief system, the world is moving towards a meaningful end, and we should align ourselves with it. Examples of this are religious end-time teachings. Judaism, Christianity, and Islam teach such a course of the world according to a divine plan. There are also similar ideas in philosophy: see the historicism of Georg Friedrich Wilhelm Hegel, who believed that world history strived for ever greater harmony. Hegel concluded that we live in the best of all histories. Writing at the time of Prussia, Hegel argued - what a surprise - that Prussia was chosen by history for greatness and should therefore be supported. Karl Marx later turned this mental map on its head and postulated historical materialism, concluding that the goal of history was a classless society and that this could be accelerated by a dictatorship of the proletariat. The Last Generation movement is currently attracting attention. It foresees an imminent end to human life on earth if we do not prevent this, using ever escalating levels of protest.

Even blatant contradictions between reality and conviction are no solution. Quite the opposite: a sectarian religious community predicts the end of the world for the year 1925[23] . In this year, Jesus is supposed to return to earth and take the believers with him to heaven. Martin's parents were living in Danzig (Gdansk since 1945) at the time. Near Danzig lies the hill of Oliva, named after the Mount of Olives in Israel, which plays a key role in Christianity. In December 1925, many of the worldwide followers of this religious community gave away their possessions because they would no longer need them in heaven. So did the followers in Danzig, who gathered on the hill in Oliva on the bitterly frosty night of December 31, 1925, and waited for midnight. It arrived. And went. And nothing happened. The believers realized that their prophecy had not been fulfilled and had to reorganize their lives with great difficulty.

Is this the end of this religious community? Far from it. In 1926, its leadership informs its followers that humanity has been given another chance to repent. The followers are called to commit themselves to their faith even more than before. And they do. What should we call such behavior that results from a mixture of oppression, defiance, fear, and loyalty? Let us call the behavior "1926ing".

But watch out! Before we make fun of this irrational behavior, we should reflect whether we ourselves do not act similarly when faced with conflicts between our personal reality tunnel and actual reality, particularly in areas that are significant to the meaning of our lives. We find examples of 1926ing all around us. Every televised political debate shows that 1926ing occurs everywhere and on all sides of socially and personally relevant issues. Take the hot topic of climate change:

Anyone who is convinced that climate change is a hoax and that all previous data on climate change are irrelevant is behaving no differently than the religious community just described. That is obviously 1926ing.

We also observe the 1926ing among those convinced of climate change: in 2018, a tweet by Greta Thunberg about a study went around the world warning that climate change would "*wipe out humanity*" if the world did not stop using fossil fuels "*by June 2023*"[24] . As a result, the convinced 1926ers no longer remember this false prophecy in 2023 ... and continue to sound the alarm for imminent climate catastrophe.

Whether we are aware of it or not, our 1926ing is an attempt to protect our Siamese Twins, reality tunnels and meaning of life, from collapsing. This does not have to be so: As we shall see, our 1926ing can be avoided through Scenario Planning Extreme.

III. The trends of the past determine the future. The goal is to calculate the future for one's own specific purposes. Sure enough: If you look for patterns in the past, you will find what you are looking for. Repeating patterns can be easily extrapolated into the future. In the short run, particularly in stable contexts, we may even be correct. The prerequisite for this, however, is that times hardly change.

The strategic planning of the Prussian General Staff was notoriously successful for around a hundred years with its approach based on extrapolations of past success. Its planning system was based on recognized, repetitive patterns during battles and wars. This approach was used repeatedly to plan, wage, and win Prussia's wars. Its greatest success was the Franco-Prussian War of 1870/71, which led to the foundation of the German Reich. However, this approach failed spectacularly during the . Why was that?

In 1914, barbed wire and machine guns, as well as new weapons for Europe on both sides of the conflict, led to years of trench warfare with millions of casualties. And it got worse. In 1916, the British tested their invention of the tank, which could overcome barbed wire and machine guns. They initially tested it with 36 units, with mixed results. After an initial panic, the Germans learned to defend themselves by firing directly at them with artillery. The Prussian General Staff also considered developing tanks but decided against it due to the initial difficulties with the new armored weapon. However, Great Britain, France, and the US continually improved upon this innovation and deployed more tanks, while the Prussian General doubled down in refusing to take the innovation seriously.

In 1918, the Western Allies deployed over ten thousand tanks. The German military was overwhelmed and offered to surrender in panic. Luckily for them, US President Woodrow Wilson agreed. Germany was thus spared a catastrophic occupation. The famous strategist General Heinz Guderian analyzed and described the German tank disaster and its years in 1926 in a remarkable book.[25]

Despite this disaster, classic strategic planning in the tradition of the Prussian General Staff often remains the order of the day and continues to be the prevailing approach even today. The German penchant for precise calculation plays a seductive role here.

Wake Up, Automotive Industry!

China has become the world's leading exporter of automobiles with electric cars[26]
, while former world automotive export champion Germany was stuck in its efforts to become a major player in electric cars, and this against the backdrop of a legislative ban on the registration of cars with combustion engines imposed by the EU as of 2035, except for still exotic e-fuels produced using renewable energy sources. 149 years of the automotive industry with combustion engines will then end in Europe. In the process, up to 800,000 current jobs as of 2022 in the German automotive industry are at risk to disappear. Europe-wide the loss of jobs could be much larger. It looks like another painful example of the dangers of 1926ing for an entire industry is unfolding before our eyes, admittedly in slow motion. Tesla and China are smiling all the way to the bank.

A personal word for our readers about 1926ing: it is easy to recognize it happening to others. Those who are firmly convinced that they are immune to it should consider whether there are areas in their own convictions that they consider rock-solid and non-negotiable. It is precisely in these areas that the probability is extremely high that conflicts between one's own Siamese Twins, the reality tunnel/meaning of life on the one hand and the "true" reality on the other will be hidden/downplayed by one's own 1926ing.

1.2
This is Scenario Planning Extreme

*It is about being
successful in every scenario
and being prepared for anything.*
Charles Hampden-Turner [27]

Scenario Planning Extreme has its origins in the US. We are in the 1960s and four major powers possess nuclear weapons. The US is thinking about how to deal with potential nuclear threats from the Soviet Union. The destructive potential of nuclear weapons is unimaginably great. And not only that. With missiles, it can reach any target on earth within a couple of hours or less, regardless of where they are launched from. This makes all the usual military planning with an over-whelming all-out counterattack on the enemy pointless. An all-our war would lead to a nuclear winter, which would mean the end of the world as we know it, and the attacker would de facto commit suicide. How does one prepare in such a completely unique environment for the various possible forms of nuclear war?

Herman Kahn[28] , founder of the world's first futurology institute, the Hudson In-stitute, develops a brilliant answer: scenario planning. If you only have about one hour to react to various attacks, then it is important to think through all types of attacks in advance and develop suitable responses for each situation. This also includes determining how the distinct types of attacks can be recognized and differentiated from one another. Scenario planning does exactly that. It makes it possible to prepare thoroughly for a wide range of eventualities to be able to react quickly and appropriately if necessary.

The oil corporation Shell discovers Herman Kahn's scenario planning and uses it during the first oil crisis in 1973.[29] v Arab oil producing and exporting countries (OPEC[30]) are angered by Western countries' military support for Israel in the Yom Kippur War and decide to drastically reduce oil production, multiply the price of oil, and nationalize the facilities of foreign oil companies in the Middle East. In these times of crisis, Germany experiences car-free highways on weekends for the first time. In the US, gas is rationed by distributing it in $5 increments on odd and even days, depending on automotive license plates.

How can an oil organization thrive in such a challenging situation? The answer for all oil companies remains consistent: seek new sources of oil globally and secure the necessary exploration and production rights. In this way, they can circumvent OPEC's supply restrictions and eventually access oil from alternative sources.

Shell does the same. However, behind closed doors it also applies the scenario planning approach[31] to ask itself: what would happen if many OPEC countries were to quietly and secretly sidestep their agreed production limits to such an extent that OPEC would decide to abandon its restrictions? This is unimaginable for many managers, and for the world at large. Why would OPEC betray its golden idea of restricting the output and increasing the price of crude oil? Unthinkable.

Shell is nevertheless exploring this issue and considers what strategic consequences would be derived from it. The answer is clear: if the OPEC countries disregard their own restrictions and sell crude oil to meet market demands, then it makes more sense for Shell to invest the money in additional oil refineries and in the expansion of its own gas station network. So, there are two scenarios: (1) The cartel remains strong and limits oil production. (2) The cartel abandons restrictions and oil becomes freely available. Each scenario has its own strategies.

The question remains as to how we would be able to recognize that OPEC's restrictions were about to be lifted. Shell's scenario team finds an answer: there is a London spot market on which excess crude oil is traded. If this price falls below the standard OPEC price by a certain amount, then the end of the oil embargo is only a matter of time and Shell should be the first to change its strategies.

A few years later, that happens. Shell is the first to act and gains billions in profits. The organization is so enthusiastic about scenario planning that it initially wants to keep this successful method exclusively for itself[32] . You cannot blame them. Fortunately, the scenario experts at Shell disagree. They are convinced that such methods should be academically researched, and they get their way.

Let us note the essentials in both cases: Neither Herman Kahn nor Shell Oil asked for probabilities of the various scenarios. Probabilities deliberately played no role. Instead, they identified indicators that showed when which scenarios would occur, and which strategies should be implemented.

Flying With One Foot on the Ground: The Scenario Method/Technique

Scenario planning has spread throughout the world since the 1980s. It has also arrived in German-speaking countries and is known there under the name Scenario method/technique[33] . On closer inspection, however, the German-language version is a hybrid of the American courage to embrace uncertainty and the German obsession with precision. At its core, it is quantitative planning based on forecasts, while also considering various qualitative trends. This leads to a "scenario funnel" for the future with a "most likely" future in the middle of the funnel, a "best case" deviation upwards, and a "worst case" deviation downwards. There is now even a DIN standard (German industrial norm) for this. The inclusion of a quantitative element in trend descriptions, with the calculation of "best case" and "worst case" scenarios, signifies a significant departure from the original approaches developed by American companies and Shell. This means that the scenario technique/method carries the risk of easily leading to drastic misjudgments by limiting the range of possible futures to those calculated as "most likely", potentially overlooking alternative outcomes that deviate significantly from these projections. It is like voluntarily choosing to put on quantitative blinders.

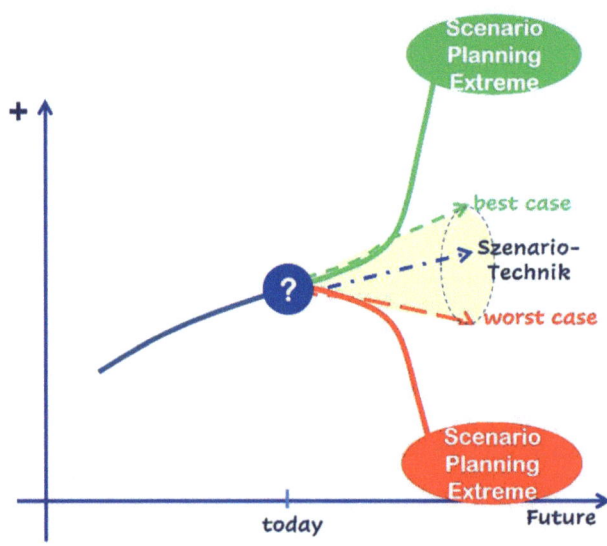

Let us think about military scenario planning. What was the probability of a nuclear attack in the sixties, and to what extent? Unpredictable. What was the likelihood of OPEC abandoning its restrictions? Unpredictable.

With all due respect, the German-language scenario method/technique seems from the outside to be an attempt to fly while keeping one foot on the ground. You cannot fly like that. Although various scenarios are thought through, the approach of quantitatively extrapolating current trends means that they remain tied to the past, i.e., the status quo.

This is precisely what makes them so popular in Germany. However, this also makes it difficult for experienced managers to question the continuity of their previous reality tunnels and openly consider other futures. Could this be one of the reasons why the German automotive industry is in danger of missing the great transition to electric cars and is about to lose it to Chinese car manufacturers like BYD? In fact, as of 2024, the EU imposed tariffs on their import as temporary defense.

Scenario planning about the potential of extreme change in electrically powered cars might have prevented this blindness to change. It could have prevented 1926ing!

Black Swans:
Big Changes Are Possible Overnight

Thanks to Nassim Nicholas Taleb[34] , we now have a name for improbable developments: black swans. With this memorable metaphor, he brought unlikely phenomena to the forefront of our time, which is characterized by ever increasing change.

Taleb reminds us: Before the discovery of Australia, the world was certain: all swans are white. With the discovery of Australia, our assumption about the color of swans went out the window. We realized that swans could be either white or black. Taleb warns us that this also applies to many areas of our lives. Reality constantly confronts us with sudden changes that we must deal with, but whose possible exponential effects we initially ignore:

Greta Thunberg and her strike for climate[35] has fundamentally changed our society. Greta turned out to be a black swan. Before her appearance, no one would have imagined that a young student could make the global climate a dominant issue of our time, with radical consequences for everyone's life. Greta sparked the global Fridays for Future movement. The Last Generation movement and individuals who protest by glueing themselves to roads would be unthinkable without her influence. Such radical change was unforeseen, and yet, in retrospect, it was only a matter of time before the climate crisis would demand everyone's attention.

The video of the tragic murder of George Floyd[36] during a demonstration in the US has turned the country upside down. It changed everything. It turned Black Lives Matter, Diversity-Equity-Integration (DEI or any iteration of those initials) and other initiatives into powerful movements that are changing US politics in ways we never expected. How predictable was it that police departments were to be partially defunded and abolished despite dramatically rising crime rates?

Historical monuments were torn down. Libraries began discarding books long regarded as masterpieces of literature. By 2023, job applicants at numerous companies in the US were only hired if they could demonstrate having the "right" attitudes. The same held true for college admissions.

Open AI's ChatGPT[37] revolutionized artificial intelligence (AI) by making it instantly available to the entire world in November 2022. In just a few months, it had over 150 million users worldwide. Some forms of AI applications had been in use for many years. ChatGPT exceeded all expectations. Other companies, such as Microsoft, Google, and Samsung, entered economic competition with AI programs of their own. A five-page business plan for an organization? No sweat: ChatGPT delivers it over the Internet in just 15 seconds.[38] It has professional level quality. A consultant could have demanded and received a high fee for this. ChatGPT also writes computer codes on request, and they work. Virtually overnight, the world is confronted with fundamental questions about the future of human labor, including ethical questions about the limits of the use of AI and the possibilities of its control in the face of competition between countries, among others. Again, there is no predictable empirical data that could have been used to anticipate this surprise.

Scenario Planning Extreme Defined

With Scenario Planning Extreme, the name says it all. Our approach goes a significant step beyond the original: We deliberately include black swan events —unpredictable occurrences that trigger exponential change—into future scenarios.

Scenario Planning Extreme is the

1 Systematic exploration and thinking through the implications of...
2 ...various extreme futures/scenarios in the long term...
3 ...based on exponentially amplifying currently visible trends to imagine the future...
4 ...as well as the development of scenario-specific success strategies...

5 ...and the identification of scenario alert signals for the implementation of scenario strategies.

1 - <u>Systematic Exploration and Examination of Implications.</u> We each experience our own unique "reality tunnels", which are shaped by our perceptions and bounded by limits that are invisible to us. These boundaries often make it easier for us to anticipate a future with minor or moderate changes than a future involving extreme shifts that might call into question our self-image and our sense of purpose in life. In **Scenario Planning Extreme**, we put our reality tunnels to the test by embarking on a deeply imaginative journey into diverse potential future worlds, exploring their details with precision. What do these futures look like? What would it feel like to live in them? We imagine vivid storyboards or impressive movie scripts for these crafted futures. By immersing ourselves in these richly textured visions, we gain the ability to experience these futures as if we could visit them and feel what it is like to live in them ourselves.

2 - <u>Various extreme future long-term scenarios.</u> There are three psychological reactions to changes in the status quo. If the perceived change seems too moderate, we assimilate it: We classify it as a mere variation of the current situation. If, on the other hand, the changes described are extreme, the so-called contrast effect occurs, and we reject the perceived change as too extreme and "unrealistic". The traditional advice for achieving acceptance of recommended changes, therefore, is the third way: to suggest change that lies *between* assimilation and the contrast effect. This is the de facto stance of the scenario method/technique.

Scenario Planning Extreme takes a different approach by deliberately exploring scenarios that provoke a contrast effect. This method challenges our reality tunnels through deliberately provoking extreme scenarios, including potential black swan events - thereby open them up to new perspectives and possibilities. In this way, we embrace and even enjoy imaginative journeys into extreme futures, legitimized by the methodology, allowing us to understand these futures in detail and thoroughly exploring their implications.

Scenario Planning Extreme typically develops four distinct scenarios, each deliberately targeting the most threatening and uncertain areas of the spectrum of possible futures. This approach ensures a broad exploration of potential outcomes, often leading participants to discover both a preferred scenario that resonates with their hopes and one that evokes their deepest fears.

Extreme scenario planning always looks 25 years into the future. The 25-year time perspective is our license to think about extremes. Everyone would agree that it is impossible to quantify societal change over a period of 25 years in advance. This impossibility frees our imagination from our preference for quantification. Of course, we should be aware that sometimes, a single year can bring as much change as would be expected over 25 years. The reverse is also thinkable.

Our experience with Scenario Planning Extreme seminars has shown that concerned and worried clients find it easier to engage with scary scenarios if it is *in the context of three others*. Consciously and playfully exploring four distinct possibilities encourages engagement with all scenarios, fostering a deeper understanding and interest in the strategies associated with each one.

3 – Imagining based on currently visible trends. The number of futures is limitless. To make them manageable, we narrow them down using various approaches. Scenario Planning Extreme begins by identifying all already visible trends that could potentially become relevant in shaping the future, regardless of how important or unimportant they may appear today.

We then imagine that the identified trends develop exponentially over a period of 25 years. The different futures that emerge in this way are radically different from the present. We study them to understand their implications, including those that we would never have thought possible but have now begun to recognize in the context of the study.

Imagine if IBM had used Scenario Planning Extreme when investigating the potential of the PC, simulating how the massive networking of PC cores might eventually challenge even its own mainframes. Could this foresight have changed the organization's strategic decisions?

Would AT&T's decision against the cell phone have been different if, through a Scenario Planning Extreme project, the company had envisioned a future world in which the cell phone evolved into a product that eventually everyone would want to own? Such a scenario might have reshaped their strategic outlook.

Could Nokia have better anticipated the transformative importance of smartphones by utilizing a Scenario Planning **Extreme** project? Such an approach might have allowed the company to explore and prepare for a future where smartphones became an essential and ubiquitous part of daily life, potentially reshaping its strategic decisions.

The answer to all three questions would be a clear "yes, and". These questions will be explored in more detail in Chapter Step 10.

4 - Development of scenario-specific success strategies. Scenario Planning Extreme is always guided by a specific goal: to maintain or strengthen the future viability of an organization. The aim to ensure success, regardless of which future becomes reality. By analyzing the unique characteristics, opportunities, and risks presented in each individual scenario, it is possible identify which strategies make sense for your own organization, determine which tactics are available to support these strategies, and devise methods to avoid or overcome obstacles to their implementation.

Scenario Planning Extreme works in the same way as strategic therapy: by deliberately exacerbating the symptoms we overcome the illness (see also Paul Watzlawick's book "The Situation is Hopeless but Not Serious[39] ").

5 - Scenario alert signals are wake-up calls for commencing with the implementation of scenario-specific strategies. We are all familiar with the metaphor of the frog jumping out of a pot of hot water. The same frog will stay in a pot of initially cool water as it gradually heats to a boil. In the context of Scenario Planning Extreme, scenario alert signals act as critical thermometers for the organizational "frog." These indicate when the temperature has reached a point that requires action, helping organizations determine the optimal time to implement the corresponding strategies. By doing so, they can ensure they are first to market and the first to reap the benefits of emerging opportunities.

Extreme Times - Extreme Change

Who has not heard of Moore's Law? It states that the performance of microchips doubles every 18 months and that their price per performance is halved.

Originally formulated partly in jest by Intel's former CEO Gordon Moore, it has been proven true for over forty years. The performance of today's smartphones and AI would not be possible without them. The consequences of Moore's law for the semiconductor industry are extreme: If a product misses the market by six months, half of the potential profits are lost.

The attitude of companies in the semiconductor industry was and is therefore to constantly pay attention to new developments, take them seriously and react to them as quickly as possible. In the semiconductor industry one is well advised to view all trends, even the smallest ones, as potentially extreme in their impact.

Andy Grove, Intel's first, much respected (and feared[40]) Chief Operating Officer, put it concisely: "Only the paranoid survive[41] ". Our book subtitle "Only going too far is going far enough" reflects this attitude. This view has enabled Intel to remain at the forefront of the creative US semiconductor industry for over sixty years.

Does this only apply to the semiconductor industry? No. As early as 2003, a German mobile phone manufacturer explained to a politician why the organization was withdrawing from the development and production of mobile phones: *"In Germany, we need 18 months to develop a new mobile phone model. In Taiwan it takes a mere six months. We cannot keep up with that.*[42]

Similarly rapid and extreme changes can now be observed in many other sectors. The extensive use of AI will further accelerate change in all areas of the economy and society. Today, Andy Grove's radical perspective is good advice for all companies.

Dear reader – This is an official invitation to Be Paranoid!

1.3
Scenario Planning Extreme
Accountability Starts with the CEO

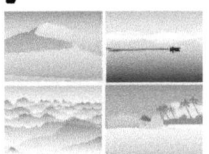

The very cave you are afraid to enter
holds what you seek the most.
Joseph Campbell [43]

*S*cenario Planning Extreme is an invitation to submit your successful reality tunnel to a stress test and thereby improve it. This is an invitation to both individuals and organizations. We recommend it to companies as well as to the public sector and politics. We are also convinced that it would help NGOs to look for new ways to initiate desired change and to be ever more effective, respected and considered.

Insights from Scenario Planning Extreme projects can lead to fundamental changes and paradigm shifts in the organizational environment that require reorientation. Completely new rules for success for your own organizational biotope can emerge in the process. At that point, Scenario Planning Extreme becomes a matter for the Chief Executive Officer (CEO), because far-reaching changes must involve the very top with the organization's self-definition, for which the CEO and the supervisory board are responsible.

This chapter will begin by examining companies that thrive on generating profits and must keep pace with constantly changing markets to ensure their survival. Next, we delve into the realms of politics and the public sector. Following this, we offer some reflections on the role and challenges of NGOs. Finally, we conclude with a discussion on the implications for individuals.

Every year, the business magazine "Fortune" publishes a list of the five hundred most successful companies. What an impressive list of successful organizations. However, a look at their longevity is sobering. The average life expectancy of a Fortune 500 organization is around 40 years. [44]

In the 1990s, books came into fashion that dealt with particularly successful companies and showed how they achieved their success. These included the book by James Collins and Jerry Porras[45] : "Built to Last: Successful Habits of Visionary Companies". The companies described in the book were praised as benchmark examples against which all other companies should be measured. These included, for example, Hewlett Packard and Xerox. Following the advice of the companies described in this book, it was fashionable for a few years. But many disappointed their readers: After just ten years, several of them had lost their exemplary character, including these two.

How do companies manage to be successful for more than 40 years? The answer to this question remained unanswered for a long time until Shell looked at companies that had been successful for more than two hundred years and asked: What enabled them to remain successful despite all the technological, social, and political changes? [46]

Shell's former head of planning, Arie de Geus, reported on the results in his remarkable book "The Living Organization"[47] . According to De Geus, "living" companies change in some areas and remain true to themselves in others. What changes are the specific products and services they offer to clients? What does not change are the values by which they operate.

Let us take TÜV[48] , the German "Association for the Control of technical products" from Cars to coffee makers which is already over 150 years old. Its forerunner was founded on January 6, 1866, as a Society for the inspection and technical safety of steam boilers after steam-powered ships repeatedly exploded due to excessive pressure of its steam boilers. Today, TÜV tests the safety of all technical products that come onto the market in Germany. For countries that export their products to Germany, TÜV even operates test centers in these countries. The testing of steam boilers is just a curious reminiscence of their origins. But the values of TÜV have remained the same: To ensure the reliability and safety of technical devices.

According to De Geus, living companies are characterized by four features:

- *"They behave sensitively towards their environment and are therefore able to learn and adapt all the time.*
- *They develop strong cohesion among employees to form a community with its own group and organizational identity.*
- *They are tolerant of innovative ideas and open to the decentralization of decisions.*
- *They are conservative when managing financing matters enabling them to control their own organizational development even in times of crisis"*[49] .

This mixture of openness to change and maintaining one's own principles is reflected in the willingness to learn. Shell sums this up with the sentence: *"In the future, our speed of learning will be our only long-term competitive advantage.*[50]

HuLiO reality tunnels

Living companies grow in good times and preserve their values and ideals even in times of crisis. De Geus puts it concisely: *"Like all organisms, the living organization exists primarily for its own survival and improvement and to become as large as possible.*[51]

In this sense, we propose to add the metaphor of organizations as human beings in our reality tunnels, analogous to us humans as acting subjects. We will call them: **Hu**man **Li**ke **O**rganization: HuLiO.

We distinguish between three types of HuLiOs:

- Commercial enterprises such as HuLiO(c),
- Political organizations HuLiO(p)
- Non-profit organizations such as NGOs HuLiO(n).

The reason for these distinctions? Different rules of success apply to diverse types of HuLiOs. Companies aim to thrive in economic competition by successfully developing and bringing innovative ideas and products to market. Political organizations seek to gain and maintain power to effectively serve the people. NGOs, on the other hand, strive for recognition and influence within society, the business world, and political arenas.

We will focus primarily on HuLiO(c) companies, as they form the economic foundation of our society. Chapter 1.4 is dedicated to the political world.

Despite the differences in the rules for success, all three types of HuLiOs will be better understood if we see, value, and treat them as human beings with a purpose of their own and a desire to develop their full potential in the long term.

An organization with a HuLiO self-image will find it easier to act in a way that increases its life expectancy. The prudent HuLiO(c) puts its employees first. Products and services come second. The question of profit and loss follows as third priority. This appears to be quite different from the thinking and actions of several companies and management consultants. In 2022, the book by Walt Bogdanich and Michael Forsythe caused a stir: "When McKinsey Comes to Town. The Hidden Influence of the World's Most Powerful Consulting Firm."[52] The book's blurb claims that McKinsey receives billions in fees from large companies and governments who ask McKinsey to show them how to maximize profits and increase efficiency in the short term[53]. The cover picture shows an empty factory floor, presumably because of the consultants' advice to improve profits by outsourcing production to companies in low labor cost countries.

We share De Geus' view that the priority is not profit or products/services, but rather the organization itself and its employees. AMD founder and former CEO Jerry Sanders stated this idea concisely: "*People come first. Products and profits will follow.*"[54]

When Proven Paradigms Are Displaced

The HuLiO perspective still is an exception for many organizations. It is tragic when companies continue to cling to their previously successful approaches using 1926ing logic???, even when all the signs point to the need for reorientation.

The consequences of change within an evolving reality landscape often results in the demise of a company's existing business paradigm. At best, this leads to its replacement by a new one. This process mirrors the well-known five stages of grief originally described by Elisabeth Kübler-Ross[55] :

- Denial
- Anger
- Negotiation
- Depression
- Acceptance.

Denial. Imagine being one of the managers at IBM who was involved in the success of the IBM mainframes. Imagine further that we were sitting in a meeting discussing Intel's initiative to kill off our successful mainframes by connecting many PC cores. It is quite possible that we would consider this idea crazy and impractical. In our view, it would be ridiculous to think for a moment that the phenomenal performance of mainframes could be rivaled by tiny input devices, let alone render them redundant.

Anger. We would be furious if this idea were to continue to be brought up and would work to ensure that this "nonsense" is no longer put on the table in the future.

Negotiation. If we cannot get rid of this idea, we might next try to urge the company to look for compromise solutions, such as combining existing mainframes and interconnected PC cores à la Intel.

Depression. Once we realize that even such suggestions are useless, depression would await us. We would mourn our wealth of experience and previous success.

Acceptance. Finally, we would accept the end of our mainframe world as we knew it. Our paradigm has died and with it our individual careers. What a pity.

This would be particularly unfortunate because the predictable end of a beloved and familiar paradigm was hidden by our reality tunnels until it was too late for a rebirth with a new paradigm.

Scenario Planning Extreme as an incubator for new success paradigms. Organizations can remain successful for centuries if they prioritize learning at the forefront of their analyses and decision-making processes. By doing so, they can uncover new learning opportunities for growth, enabling themselves to anticipate critical changes and develop innovative solutions, ready to act when triggered by appropriate scenario alert signals. This is the transformative potential of Scenario Planning Extreme. It demonstrates that even the most threatening scenarios are worth exploring, as they can often reveal unexpected opportunities for advancement and resilience.

Secret Ingredient: Co-Ownership

How can I motivate other people? By making them co-owners and transforming _my_ decisions into _our_ decisions. This is the secret ingredient for all successful long-term change. We all want to see ourselves as acting subjects, not as objects being manipulated by others. Co-ownership is the surest way to self-motivation, a principle that applies universally at all levels, whether to top managers or receptionists.

Those who see their organizations as HuLiO also recognize that learning holds greater value than static knowledge. When a proven success formula is threatened, the right response should be to enhance it or even discover a completely new one. Let us embrace the ideal fast learning. And since learning inevitably involves making mistakes, one guiding principle stands out: let us make mistakes faster than our competitors, combined with the hope that we strive to ensure that every mistake is a new one.

Scenario Planning Extreme is a tool for rapid learning in a playful way, in which we put ourselves into possible, imagined extreme scenarios. We put our previously successful reality tunnels to the stress test. We may recognize that they will no longer be successful in an extremely changed future. We playfully avoid the Kübler-Ross stages of grief in paradigm death by instead co-discovering, co-inventing, co-designing, co-deciding, and co-supporting new success paradigms. We are thus becoming co-owners in the process.

Organizational learning and decision making go hand in hand at a HuLiO. Learning is always also the learning of the decision-makers because they decide whether to implement new strategies. And they will do so when they become part of the team that defined and fine-tuned them.

Merely presenting innovative solutions to decision-makers without first involving them can easily lead to temporary astonishment followed by retreat to familiar "tried and true" business approaches. Unfortunately, this is the typical reaction in many organizations when employees bring back innovative ideas from external seminars. To overcome this hurdle, decision-makers must be actively engaged in the development of innovative ideas. Only by drawing them into innovative ideas as active co-creators do they become co-owners of the new concepts. This fosters the motivation and commitment needed to make the necessary decisions for successful implementation.

Scenario Planning Extreme: A Journey in Ten Steps

1 - The Team: Scenario Planning Extreme is always a team project. Just as it is best to climb a high mountain together with partners, it is best to think about futures in a team with interested volunteers. Anyone planning such a project should therefore also think about who belongs to the team. Originally, scenario planning was primarily conducted by teams of experts. However, there is no reason a dedicated group of committed volunteers, bringing diverse perspectives and working collaboratively, could not achieve equally successful outcomes.

2 - The Client: The question of the future is always also the question of "for whom". In the second step of the Scenario Planning Extreme journey, we clarify who the HuLiO client is, what values determine their corporate identity and what their purpose for existence is.

3 - The Key Question: Scenario Planning Extreme is always guided by a specific, strategic question posed by the client.

4 - Trends: The starting points for exploring futures lies in the many currently visible trends – regardless of their scale - across politics, the economy, the environment, society, and technology. These trends are examined for their potential impact on the strategic question in focus.

5 - From Trends to Scenarios: Trends can lead to extreme changes in 25 years through exponential growth or decline. We imagine these changes and discover patterns for different scenarios. Trends are the building blocks of scenarios. The trends with the most dramatic effect on the key question will be used as cornerstones for imagining four different scenarios.

6 - Storyboards: For each scenario we develop gripping and lively storyboards that make the scenarios come alive for the client.

7 - <u>Strategies:</u> Each scenario calls for tailored strategies that ensure the client's success within that specific context. These strategies are supported by a series of step-by-step include several tactics designed to effectively address the unique challenges and opportunities of each scenario.

8 – <u>Scenario Alert Signals</u>: Scenarios are not predictions. That is why it is crucial to identify signals that serve as early warnings when one of the scenarios begin to unfold in reality- These signals indicate that the time has come to activate and implement the strategies planned for that specific scenario.

9 – <u>Winning Over the Client:</u> Recommendations only count if they are accepted. The aim of this step is to win the client over by gaining their confidence and commitment to the proposed scenarios and their associated strategies.

It is often most effective to first give the client and their decision-makers the opportunity to test their existing successful strategies within the imagined scenarios—and see them fail. Allowing time for reflection helps to create an openness to exploring new strategies for success, as De Geus observed during his work at Shell[56] . This critical phase is typically skipped over in external seminars.

10 – <u>Implementation:</u> How can the client effectively implement their decisions? What new responsibilities arise for whom – either for specific individuals or teams? How can the client regularly update the studies and communicate them to employees as part of a rapid innovation process?

How to Involve Decision-Makers

Just as a stone thrown into a lake creates ripples that spread across the entire lake, Scenario Planning Extreme can start anywhere in an organization. The goal is to enable the decision-makers to develop trust in the approach by familiarizing them with the process, engaging them, and transforming them into co-creators and co-owners. This involves two key aspects: first, fostering ownership of the scenarios and the new strategies for success, and second, positioning Scenario Planning Extreme as a valuable tool for preparing for all possible futures. Here is a sequence of steps:

- **Presentation**: Begin with a presentation introducing the Scenario Planning Extreme approach.

- **Seminar for Employees**: Conduct a seminar for employees from the client's planning or organizational development team, focusing on an external issue unrelated to the organization. A proven method in our seminars is to simulate a scenario where participants are tasked by the EU Commission to develop success strategies for a topic that could shape the future of the EU 25 years from now. This approach is both exciting and non-binding for the client. The seminar format follows the ten steps previously described.
- **Pilot Project with a Volunteer Trendsetter**: Identify a volunteer trendsetter within the client's organization who is willing to carry out a pilot project in their area of responsibility. This serves as a demonstration of the usefulness of the approach for the organization. Our experience has shown that organizations are more receptive and willing to initially try out a radical new idea within a limited scope before considering immediate wider implementation for the entire organization. The pilot project format also follows the ten-step framework.
- **Expansion Through Additional Pilot Projects**: Use the results of the initial pilot project to identify more trendsetters within the organization. These additional pilot projects further demonstrate the usefulness of the approach and its potential for broader application throughout the whole organization.
- **Organizational Study**: A study for the entire organization can start with a specific topic affecting only part of it. The speed of acceptance of the approach is less critical than building the growing confidence of key decision-makers. Drawing on Daniel Kahneman's distinction between fast and slow thinking, when addressing long-term strategic challenges, adopting a slow-thinking approach is the surest way to achieve greater sustained success[57] .

1.4
Scenario Planning Extreme
in Politics

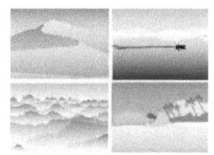

The basic assumption in any democracy is that
within the limits of the constitution
the voter is always right.[58]
Martin Gillo

*S*cenario Planning Extreme is a valuable tool for political organizations to prepare for potential substantial change. While the ten-step process remains the same as that used in corporations—the primary focus of this book—political organizations differ from the business world in several ways:

While timing is important in business, it is even more critical in politics, where there are less tangible "products or services" to deliver. In business, the goal is to produce and provide products or services as efficiently as possible to meet client needs, aligning with the Greek concept of kronos (chronological time). However, in politics, the focus is on delivering policies, decisions, and actions that shape societal structures, address public needs, and influence collective well-being. Because these outcomes are often intangible and prioritized around implementing ideas and principles that affect people's lives, the focus shifts to kairos—the "right time"—where success often hinges on presenting the right idea or action at the perfect moment. Although timing matters in both contexts, the nuanced

49

difference lies in politics' greater reliance on aligning actions to seize opportune moments for social impact. Julia Bonk, 18 years old at the time and freshly elected to the Saxony State Parliament for the Party for Democratic Socialism (PDS), experienced this firsthand, and got to feel this painfully. In 2004, she proposed the legalization of marijuana and heroin[59]—a suggestion that was met with ridicule and outright dismissal by both politicians and the media as unrealistic. Martin, while intrigued by the proposal and open to discussion, chose to remain silent, deeming it politically wiser to avoid being drawn into the media spectacle. This topic is revisited again in Chapter 3.3 examined from the perspective of Scenario Planning Extreme.

In politics, the iron law of avoiding mistakes and never admitting them reigns supreme. While entrepreneurs are often admired for their courage, boldness, and willingness to take risks, politicians and public administration officials risk long-term credibility if they pursue daring or high-stake risks. As a result, a cautious and measured approach is essential when applying Scenario Planning Extreme in the political arena.

The power of the party leadership, even in democratic parties, can be compared with the power of an emperor in an absolutist monarchy. For instance, the German Chancellor has the authority to dismiss any minister from their party in the cabinet overnight, even with a simple telephone call, if they choose to do so. While the German Chancellor has the discretion to appoint successors, the executive authority of the U.S. President is even broader, highlighting the considerable concentration of power at the highest levels of leadership.

Political scenario planning is therefore usually initiated by the top leadership. Gaining the support of relevant decision-makers is crucial to exploring innovative ideas. Whether and to what extent such a project "makes sense" in politics depends on the perspective of those in charge. True exploration can only begin once a decision from the top has been made.

In a democracy, political leaders serve as the only representatives of the sovereign: the voters. In Scenario Planning Extreme projects that affect society, it is essential to gradually draw voters into a meaningful societal dialogue with politicians. This fosters greater engagement, collaboration, and alignment between policy makers and the public they serve.

From 2004 to 2007, the topic of demographic developments was on everyone's mind in the State of Saxony. In response, the Saxony State Parliament set up a commission of inquiry to address these developments, with Martin serving as a member. During its first meeting, the commission agreed to a request from the ruling coalitions to maintain confidentially regarding its ongoing work and results, opting to share its findings only at one single final press conference.

This happened after three years in parliament and briefly made headlines –For just two days. Three years of painstaking work quickly disappeared from political and public discourse. A genuine dialogue with the sovereign–the voters– would have looked vastly different. It would have made a lot more sense to keep the public informed about the commission's monthly consultations and the resulting progress, thus maintaining an ongoing dialogue with the voters. This approach could have turned the challenges of Saxony's demographic developments—and the potential opportunities for successfully overcoming them—into a sustained topic of media coverage. Only through such continuous public debate can voters be drawn into the conversation, fostering engagement on key issues and lending legitimacy to subsequent political decisions.

Such public debate would have increased the pressure for action within the administration to find solutions for demographic changes. Remarkably, even as late as 2023, some department heads within Saxony's State ministries still appeared unwilling to acknowledge the significant demographic changes occurring within Saxony society! [60]

Coincidences often play a key role. For instance, in the case of Saxony's demographic developments, alongside the Enquete Commission established by the State parliament, the Saxony State government decided to conduct its own study on the topic. It had this study drawn up by a separate commission of experts in the field, and was strategically timed to be presented to the public shortly before the State Parliament Commission published its findings. The government's aim appeared to be to overshadow the parliament's work, claiming the spotlight for itself, or in other words to "steal the parliament's thunder".

But chance threw a spanner in the works, delivering a stark lesson in political reality. In preparation for the presentation of its findings, the government's commission had recruited high-ranking politicians from all over Germany to attend the event at the International Congress Center Dresden (ICD). National media outlets and television stations were invited, and all the prerequisites seemed perfectly aligned for broad publicity and extensive media coverage. Yet, the night before the press conference, an unexpected incident derailed these plans. Mario M., a notorious convicted sex offender, escaped from his prison cell in Dresden, climbed onto the prison roof, and threatened to jump. The dramatic standoff kept the media—and the entire nation—riveted in suspense for over 24 hours, until he finally gave himself up. Continuous live coverage of the event left no room to report on the government's press conference about demographic developments, effectively eclipsing what was planned to be a landmark moment. [61]

In politics it is said that something has only truly taken place if the media report on it. In this sense, the results and recommendations of the government commission effectively never happened. The lack of media coverage meant the findings failed to gain traction, resulting in no significant political action or far-reaching changes to address the challenges of demographic change.

In politics, only issues considered relevant by actual voters are prioritized by politicians. This has obvious implications for a Scenario Planning Extreme study in politics: it is crucial to involve voters in significant shifts in perspective. One such pilot project, "Saxony 2025" led by Martin for the Saxony State Ministry of Economics and Labor, was guided by Charles Hampden-Turner. He proposed a creative and impactful way to engage the public urging that the publicly funded State Broadcasting TV channel MDR should produce a four-part mini-series, presenting the four scenarios developed by the project team about Saxony in 2025[62] . This approach would have provided a tangible and accessible means of involving the sovereign–the voters–in shaping Saxony's future.

Finally, it must be considered that politics achieves its goals indirectly, primarily through incentivizing or regulating desired changes. It does this by changing the societal "rules of the game" through incentives, regulatory restrictions, and proposals. These tools shape behavior and guide outcomes, as we will explore in more detail later.

Non-profit NGOs

For non-governmental organizations (NGOs), similar principles apply as they do to companies. NGOs achieve their goals by influencing companies and political organizations. Unlike political entities, however, NGOs lack the authority to dictate change and can only make recommendations, even if they aspire to reach the same level of influence through high-profile campaigns.

For NGOs, participation in Extreme Scenario Planning projects conducted by business and politics can represent an ideal opportunity to have their perspectives heard, considered, and integrated into decision-making processes. Additionally, NGO representatives can successfully position themselves as contributors to such political projects in politics, provided they understand and respect the unique dynamics and rules of politics outlined earlier.

1.5
The Learning Organization

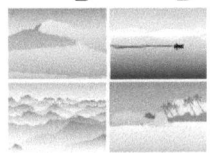

Life is the art of drawing
without an eraser.
John W. Gardner [63]

*E*very organization that defines itself as a HuLiO regards its own sustainable future as a top priority. Such organizations are aware of the constant changes in their environment and, as a result, always strive to continuous learning and improvement, refining their "reality tunnels" to adapt effectively.

In this chapter, we explore Peter M. Senge's key thoughts on the characteristics of learning organizations, as outlined in his book "The Fifth Discipline: The Art and Practice of the Learning Organization"[64] . While it is impossible to fully capture the depth of this remarkable work in just a few pages, this chapter its essential ideas. Senge's book has served—and continues to serve—as both an inspiration and roadmap to success for countless organizations striving to thrive in a dynamic world.

In his book, Senge argues that lasting success can only be achieved by companies that demonstrate the ability and willingness to keep pace with constant change, recognize the associated advantages, and exploit them for their own benefit.

What defines a learning organization? Senge postulates that it is characterized by the application of five core management disciplines, all of which must be practiced simultaneously to achieve lasting success. He further elaborates on the type of organizational atmosphere in which these principles can best flourish and thrive to reach their full potential.

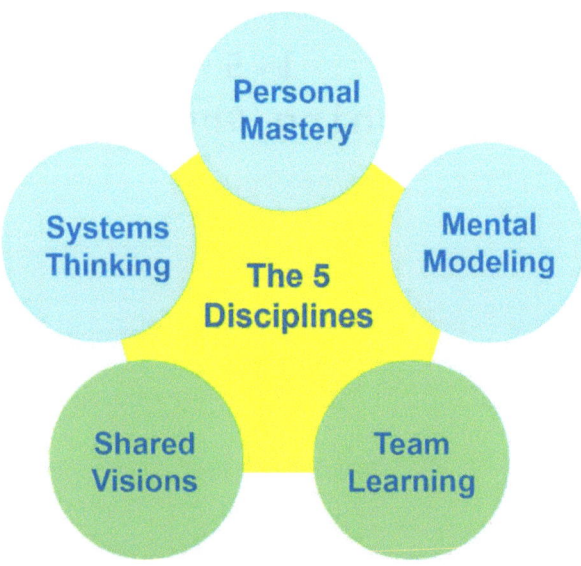

This image makes it easy to memorize the five disciplines. The top three circles represent the disciplines that are practiced individually:

(1) **Systems Thinking**: *Focusing on whole systems instead of getting lost in isolated facets of detail.*

(2) **Personal Mastery**: *Continuously striving for self-improvement rather than resting on one's laurels.*

(3) **Mental Models**: *Treating knowledge and assumptions as working hypotheses rather than set in stone.*

The two lower circles emphasize teamwork and group dynamics:

(4) **Shared Vision**: *Building a collective sense of purpose alignment with the team.*

(5) **Team Learning**: *Encouraging collaboration and dialogue to enhance collective intelligence and shared insights.*[65]

Systems Thinking[66]

Systems Thinking enables us to see and understand our world from a fresh perspective. It emphasizes the importance of long-term trends over short-term fluctuations and highlights the fact that we are all part of interconnected, complex adaptive systems that influence and depend on each other. This perspective extends to our business partners, our competitors, and our other stakeholders, acknowledging their roles within the broader system.

What does this shift in perspective achieve? Systems thinking transforms how we analyze problems, make decisions, and approach relationships, fostering a more holistic and sustainable way of thinking. We recognize that we are all part of the problem—and therefore also part of the solution. This understanding encourages us to consider the entire system, not just our own piece of it (such as our own job or department). By focusing on the bigger picture, we look for holistic, meaningful solutions, rather than just convenient cosmetics and superficial fixes. A good example of systemic thinking is the concept of the economy as a cycle, beginning with raw materials and ending with effective recycling.

For Peter Senge, this systemic approach is the essence of the "fifth discipline", which he identifies as the cornerstone of the learning organization. Its discovery was key to unlocking the potential for continuous learning and adaptation in organizations. In his book, Senge presents a series of system archetypes that enable us to better understand and influence complex systems. As in nature, momentous change can often be achieved through small, well-placed adjustments. Think of sailing: A skilled sailor can navigate the world by skillfully harnessing the existing wind—an elegant demonstration of working with, rather than against, the system.

Senge also recommends simulating strategic business decisions in advance to better understand their potential outcomes and impacts. Scenario Planning Extreme is ideal for this purpose—offering a structured approach to explore and prepare for a range of possible futures!

Personal Mastery[67]

From the most scientific to the most personal discipline: **personal mastery**. According to the American author John W. Gardner, exploring human motivation often reveals a fascinating paradox: we are simultaneously driven by a desire for stability and a longing for growth and transformation. This duality shapes how we approach challenges, opportunities, and our journey toward continuous self-improvement. We often encounter a paradox when studying human motivation: On the one hand ...

We have to face the fact that most men and women out there in the world of work are staler than they know, more bored than they would care to admit. Boredom is the secret ailment of large-scale organizations.

And yet...

You have within you more resources of energy than have ever been tapped, ... more talent than has ever been exploited, more strength than has ever been tested, more to give than you have ever given.[68]

How do you make the transition from boredom to a life in which you work to focus on personal growth? The answer begins with finding and embracing the meaning of your life. It is everyone's responsibility to give meaning to their own life. It starts with defining their own life's purpose by uncovering the values, hopes, and ideals that make their efforts and commitment feel meaningful and worthwhile. And from where does the motivation arise for that? Just as stage fright gives the actress the energy needed for her performance, motivation is fueled by the ***creative tension*** between our aspirations and the currently perceived reality. This tension, far from being a source of discomfort, becomes a driving force that propels us toward bridging the gap between where we are and where we want to be.

That is merely one side, the first half of the motivational picture. The other half lies in the deep, unspoken powerful sense of insecurity or feeling of worthlessness that we all experience—whether we admit them to ourselves or not! And these emotions can significantly narrow our potential, acting as barriers that confine us within self-imposed boundaries. As John Gardner aptly states, our fears can practically turn into our own prison.

Peter Senge challenges us to confront these inner conflicts, which often contradict the confident and capable image we frequently outwardly project. But if we look inward with honesty, we may find that such feelings are almost universal. If you believe that you are entirely free from these fears, then you might be the only one in ten thousand people who truly is. Paradoxically, the more successful we become and the closer we get to realizing our visions, the greater the tension between our aspirations and our darkest fears can grow. This heightened tension can easily leave us feeling stuck, halfway on our journey between our goals to success and the freedom to fully embrace them. It is this interplay of light and shadow within us that often defines the journey to true success and fulfillment.

How can we free ourselves from these limiting fears? And is it even possible for us to free ourselves completely from them? Peter Senge does not think so. But he shows two powerful ways to help us navigate through which we can continue to work on ourselves. Firstly, **awareness** is key. By consciously acknowledging and controlling these fears, we strip them of their power, and they get smaller. Just as pulling back a curtain and looking behind, like in the movie the Wizard of Oz: once Dorothy saw the intimidating wizard was just an old man speaking into a microphone, she became less scared. Similarly, when we examine our fears closely, they often become far less overwhelming and may even diminish.

The second approach is to cultivate our **resolve**–a steadfast commitment to pursuing our personal visions. This resolve helps us focus on our aspirations and keeps us moving forward, even in the face of fear. Together, awareness and determination create a pathway for continual growth and self-mastery, enabling us to move closer to our goals while learning to live alongside our fears.

Mental Models[69]

The third discipline, **mental models**, deals with the way we "see" the world, focusing on howe we perceive and interpret it. The real world is so vast, complex, and chaotic that it is impossible for us to fully comprehend it. To navigate this overwhelming flood of information, we construct simplified internal representations, which Peter Senge calls mental models. In our terminology, we use the term **reality tunnels** after Timothy Leary. In our way of thinking, the "walls" of our reality tunnels are made up from our mental models or maps–composed of beliefs, opinions, and insights. These mental maps provide us with a structured and simplified view of the world that makes sense to us in a way that feels coherent and manageable. However, their accuracy can vary. Sometimes our mental maps closely reflect the reality of the real-world landscape, helping us to navigate it effectively. Other times, they distort reality, limiting our ability to understand and cope with the world around us. Recognizing and refining these mental maps is essential for developing a clearer and more adaptive understanding of reality.

As long as we remain aware that all our knowledge is shaped by and reflects our mental models or maps–simplifying and sometimes distorting working hypotheses–we remain open to refining and improving them. Mental models/maps can range from global assumptions (e.g., "the tabloid press always exaggerates") to highly specific beliefs (e.g., this is how and the only way things work in our industry"). Where can problems arise?

Mental models, or reality tunnels, act as filters through which we perceive the ever-changing world. They help us to pay special attention to one thing while confidently ignoring another. However, if we regard these maps as fixed and unchangeable, we risk overlooking critical changes—particularly those that often start out small, subtly, or gradually.

A former classmate of Martin's began his career in the early 1970s at a corporation famous for manufacturing electrical and mechanical typewriters. During his tenure, one of the corporation's engineers developed an electronic typewriter and proposed it for production. Unfortunately, the management at the corporation was "sure" that electronics were only a short-term fad and that *"clients would always want mechanical typewriters."* Disillusioned, the engineer left the company, started her own business, and successfully developed electronic typewriters for companies in East Asia. Today, that formerly famous corporation exists only as a distant memory[70] .

This brings us to the greatest pitfall and main sin of all experience and mental models or maps: if we cling to them for too long, they become a paralyzing burden. Peter Senge advises us to avoid this trap, reminding us to always remain aware mental maps are mere representations and not reality itself! To avoid stagnation, we must treat mental models/maps as working hypotheses—flexible tools for understanding, rather than fixed truths. While being educated at school, college, and university, this mindset of questioning and adapting to maintain a personal perspective often comes naturally. But as we achieve greater success in our professional lives, it becomes increasingly more to maintain this openness by continuing to understand and treat our own mental models/maps as hypotheses. The third discipline, therefore, is about **thinking about thinking**–cultivating the ability to critically examine and continuously refine our mental frameworks. This self-awareness is key to staying adaptable and aligned with a world in constant change.

Shared Vision[71]

If this discipline needed a motto, the saying "United we stand. Divided we fall" would come to mind. Individually, we are in a losing position and therefore face limitations, but together, we hold the power to achieve remarkable success. Shared visions for a brighter future can inspire and energize a team—or even an entire organization—toward success. One iconic example is the world-famous vision formulated by President Kennedy in 1963: "*to put a man on the moon and bring him safely back to earth before the end of the decade*". This bold and unifying goal captured the imagination of a nation and drove extraordinary collaboration, innovation, and achievement.

What exactly is a vision? Peter Senge defines it as an attractive picture of the future that we aspire to create together, despite all the obstacles in our path. A vision usually has a time horizon of 5 to 10 years and should be deeply embedded in an organization's social mission, representing its long-term contribution to society.

Examples of profound social missions include the 1000-year construction of Cologne Cathedral and the Matsushita's 250-year commitment in Japan to end world hunger. Beyond its alignment with a social mission, a vision should be also grounded in positive core values, reflecting how the organization intends to treat its employees, clients, competitors, society, the environment, and one another.

Does an organization's vision always have to start at the top? No, not necessarily. A powerful vision can also emerge from the middle of the organization, gaining momentum and inspiring change from within.

Visions rarely originate from strategic planning departments. Why is that? Most thinking about the future begins by examining the present and the past trends that have shaped it. This backward-looking approach often unconsciously limits the organization to refining or improving what already exists. This mindset stifles the ability to envision bold, revolutionary directions, making transformative leaps impossible. True vision requires breaking free from the constraints of current paradigms and daring to imagine entirely new possibilities.

Senge's fourth discipline "**shared vision**," places a strong emphasis on commonality. And how can that happen —how can a shared vision be created? Can the CEO solemnly present their own vision and expect everyone to simply agree? No, of course not. The process starts by encouraging everyone to identify their own personal visions. A leader's vision cannot motivate others because it does not belong to them, so it is not their vision. The next step is to collaboratively shape and frame a shared vision that is compatible and aligns with the individual visions. We need to become co-creators. Only when the vision is genuinely shared will it inspire and drive the organization forward. Only this will spur us all on. Only then will we identify with our organization, enabling individuals to truly connect with their collective purpose.

Incidentally, shared visions are not static products; they are dynamic, living processes. Through ongoing dialogue and collaboration, they continually evolve, revealing ever better ways to implement goals and adapt to an ever-changing environment. This adaptability ensures that the shared vision remains relevant, vibrant, and motivating over time.

Shared visions turn from mere abstract theory to tangible real life when we recognize the discrepancy or gap between vision and the reality of our current circumstances. This **creative tension**, as Senge calls it, is essential for progress. It drives us to bridge the divide between where we are and where we want to be. This also means: a commitment to face the full truth and the willingness to be radically open to updating our mental models or maps, through continuous learning and adaptation.

Team Learning[72]

Peter Senge poses a thought-provoking question: *"How can a team of dedicated managers with an individual intelligence quotient of over 120, have a group IQ of 63?"*[73] To find the answer you only need to look at how most teams operate: Decisions are often reduced to the lowest common denominator or reflect the opinion of the most successful or dominant voice in the group. Team discussions frequently resemble an intellectual tennis match, with arguments volleying back and forth, flying around the room like tennis balls until someone finds and delivers a "killer blow" that silences the others. The insights and contributions of the losing participants are usually dismissed and often immediately forgotten entirely. As a result, many of these "losing" members may withhold their ideas in the future discussions, further stifling creativity and collaboration. This dynamic can significantly diminish a team's collective intelligence and its capacity to generate innovative solutions.

Senge advises us to make a clear distinction between **discussion** and **dialogue**. Discussions are well-suited in scenarios that the author Daniel Kahneman[74] characterizes as requiring **fast thinking**—situations where swift decisions are necessary. While dialogue is best suited in circumstances that call for Kahneman's **slow thinking**, enabling teams to learn and grow, offering the best chance to shed light on complex situations and tackle complex challenges collaboratively.

In dialogue, the team has the best opportunity to illuminate multifaceted situations collectively. The diversity of members' perspectives enables the whole team to gain better insights that surpass those of even the most competent and capable individual team member. Unlike discussions, which often focus solely on exchanging factual arguments, dialogue encourages members to share the underlying reality **tunnels**—their mental models or maps— that shape their ideas and upon which their arguments are based. However, effective dialogue requires a genuine diversity of perspectives and, critically, a willingness among team members to engage openly with and learn from the mental maps of others.

How do we create the right conditions for meaningful dialogue within the team? Peter Senge suggests three essential guidelines:

1. **Disclose Mental Models**: All team members must be prepared and willing to disclose their mental models or maps. This is best achieved by treating them as working hypotheses rather than immutable facts or unchangeable truths.

2. **Foster Collegiality**: Participants must regard each other as equals. Collegiality is an essential prerequisite for open dialogue; without it, valuable information may be withheld. A lack of equality also runs the risk that team members, consciously or unconsciously, defer to superiors who subtly signal, even unintentionally. They thereby anticipate what they believe the leader would like to hear, rather than contributing honestly.

3. **Engage a Skilled Moderator**: Dialogue thrives under the guidance of a skilled moderator who keeps the process going and ensures the process remains productive. This person should serve as a role model exemplifying openness, guaranteeing a supportive atmosphere, and keeping the conversation flowing constructively.

By following these principles, teams can create a safe and collaborative space for dialogue, enabling deeper understanding, creative solutions, and mutual growth.

How do we overcome the barriers to open dialogue? The key lies in building mutual trust between team members. Trust creates the foundation for supporting each other in talking openly about our own "**defensive routines**"—the habits and behaviors we use to protect ourselves from discomfort or vulnerability. Peter Senge notes that the force tied up in these routines, once liberated, can be redirected to unleash a lot of energy to accelerate team learning and foster collaboration.

Team learning is not an innate skill; it must be developed and practiced, much like swimming. Simply talking about it is insufficient and potentially useless. Teams wishing to seriously cultivate learning as a skill are recommended to start with a two-to-three-day seminar held outside the organization. This dedicated time and neutral environment help create space for teams to engage deeply, break down barriers, and develop the practices necessary for effective team learning.

How Do We Create A Learning Organization?[75]

How can we overcome internal tensions and other hurdles on the journey to becoming a learning organization? Peter Senge offers some valuable insights and practical suggestions to guide us along the way.

Supportive openness: Learning involves stepping outside our comfort zone. This means trying out new behaviors, talking openly about our own weaknesses, and critically examining old habits and "conventional wisdom" for their value and relevance in the future. If I want to truly improve, then I must observe myself with honesty and a willingness to grow. The key to this process lies in supportive openness— the encouragement, as well as the constructive challenges we receive from colleagues and teams that we like, trust, and respect. This dynamic fosters a positive environment where growth becomes a shared journey. However, achieving this requires the cultivation of mutual trust—and plenty of it. Trust is the foundation that allows openness to flourish and transforms challenges into opportunities for learning.

<u>Open-mindedness:</u> Peter Senge cautions: '*Nothing undermines openness more than certainty*'[76] . If I believe I know everything for sure, with absolute certainty, then I become resistant to revising my opinions and findings or embracing new perspectives. But, if I regard every insight as a working hypothesis rather than a fixed truth, then I continue to remain open to new insights, ideas, and fresh discoveries. This shift in mindset is particularly challenging for experienced managers, whose established insights seem to have always stood the test of time. Beware of managers who do not tolerate any diverging input from their colleagues. These managers risk stifling creativity and innovation within their teams. Cultivating open-mindedness is a crucial step toward fostering a learning organization and ensuring long-term success.

Two key ideas that may help to foster open-mindedness: firstly, while my beliefs and insights may still hold true today, they may be too narrow to address the complexities and challenges of the future. Recognizing this allows for greater flexibility and openness to growth. Secondly, for most strategic issues, there is rarely one single "best answer." Instead, the "best" or most effective solutions arise in a lively team exchange of diverse perspectives, emerging through dynamic team collaboration. By embracing these principles, we can move beyond rigid certainty and cultivate a culture of innovation and adaptability.

<u>Delegate decisions:</u> *"People learn fastest when they are convinced that they are responsible for their actions".*[77] With this in mind, who should make decisions? Peter Senge suggests entrusting decision-making to those with the most knowledge and commitment to the matter at hand. This approach not only empowers individuals but also ensures decisions are informed by expertise and engagement. Welcome to the age of delegating! We only need control from headquarters for decisions that affect the entire organization. For everything else, empowering those closest to the matter fosters accountability, accelerates learning, and drives better outcomes across the organization.

<u>Control without controlling:</u> Doesn't consistent delegation risk leading to chaos? Peter Senge refers to this concern with an analogy of the human body: when we catch a cold, it is not the brain's task to wake up and micromanage the immune system. Instead, the immune system operates autonomously, fighting the pathogens independently. The same principle applies in organizations—autonomous teams can effectively address local challenges without constant oversight from headquarters. But how do we, at the head office, learn to trust these "other" decentralized teams? Trust is built through clear communication, alignment on

shared goals, and confidence in the expertise and commitment of the teams. By fostering a culture of mutual accountability and providing the necessary support and resources, organizations can achieve "control without controlling ", a balance that allows for both autonomy and coordination.

This approach is exemplified by the Johnson & Johnson Group, which operates 116 companies in fifty-nine countries. The role of management in this decentralized system is to actively involve all levels of the organization in the ongoing development and confirmation of the shared vision and corporate mission. The **five disciplines of the learning organization** emerge as essential leadership and management tools for the future. Through these disciplines, committed decentralized teams, involved in continuous dialogue, are empowered to best carry out their tasks successfully. Their efforts contribute not merely to their own immediate objectives, but also for the benefit of the whole organization.

The new leader: What role remains for the leader to play in the learning organization? Peter Senge begins reframes the question with another: "*Who has the leadership role on a ship?*[78] Our spontaneous answer usually instinctively suggests that this is often "the captain". However, Senge highlights a distinct perspective: the true leader is the person who designed the ship! The **designer of the ship** is the one who defines its purpose, structure, what the ship will look like, its size, its speed, the arrangement of the functions, shaping its very essence. In the context of a learning organization, the leader adopts the role of the new supervisor. Mirroring the ship designer, the leader becomes a **designer, trainer, advisor, and mentor** for teams. They focus on creating the conditions for success, ensuring that the team's shared vision aligns with the organization's overarching vision. By fostering commitment and providing teams with significant autonomy, the leader enables the team members to develop innovative and effective solutions to their challenges. This approach shifts the leader' s role from directive authority to one of empowering and equipping the team to thrive.

Nobody is perfect: Mistakes, disappointments and short-term setbacks are inevitable parts of any learning process. To learn and grow, we must be willing to take risks. But, if an organization punishes or ridicules individuals for honest mistakes every time, it stifles innovation and discourages risk-taking. Why should anyone take risks for a better future in such an environment? A true learning organization practices the most unusual and vital principle of all healing: "*Genuine forgiveness also means ... Forgetting.*"[79] By fostering a culture of forgiveness and moving past mistakes, organizations create an environment where individuals feel safe to experiment, innovate, and pursue meaningful progress without fear of retribution. This approach turns errors into opportunities for growth rather than barriers to success.

Even the big mistakes? Yes—and there is more to consider. Peter Senge encourages us to recognize that the greater the risk, the more we should test and simulate our strategies in advance. This approach minimizes potential harm while still allowing us to take bold steps forward. Effective simulation techniques have been around for years, and modern technology, including computer-based simulations, has made them even more accessible and powerful. Just as the first time we drive a car is with a driving instructor in a safe parking lot rather than on a busy highway, organizations must consistently" practice" by playing through critical decisions and scenarios before implementing them. This method not only reduces the likelihood of costly mistakes but also fosters a culture of thoughtful risk-taking and preparedness.

The Learning Organization provides an ideal environment for **Scenario Planning Extreme** and the practical application of the five disciplines. It fosters a safe space where even the most daunting and threatening scenarios can be explored, tested, and played out without fear, enabling teams to learn, adapt, and innovate effectively. This synergy between Scenario Planning Extreme and the Learning Organization enhances both the organization's preparedness for the future and its ability to grow through continuous learning.

1.6
The Power of
Multiple Reality Tunnels

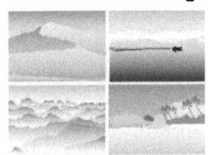

Never grow up.
Media Lab, MIT

O ne day, one of Martin's superiors at AMD Europe confronted him: "*Martin, you always tell me that you're my friend. And then you contradict me. How can you be my friend if you contradict me?*[80] Martin replied: "*Giuliano, I contradict you because I am your friend and I want to help you make the right decisions. You already have enough friends who always agree with you.*" Giuliano laughed and agreed. This exchange highlights the value of diverse perspectives. Since our individual reality tunnels can only ever capture and reflect a part of the truth, we need thoughtful, caring partners with their own distinct perspectives. By comparing and challenging each other's respective reality tunnels or differing views, we can refine and improve our understanding together. How can we best foster this kind of dynamic in a seminar?

Group Dynamics, Flow and FlowTeam Dynamics

The format and rules of such a seminar follow the principles of three foundational approaches to learning: Group Dynamics; the Success Principles of Flow, as formulated by Mihaly Csikszentmihalyi; and the extension of the flow principles to teamwork through FlowTeam Dynamics, which was developed by Swiss consultant Martin Gerber. The following sections will explore these three principles in greater detail, illustrating how they shape an effective seminar experience.

1. **Group Dynamics**[81] emphasize the critical role of interpersonal interactions, fostering mutual understanding, collaboration, and the constructive exchange of ideas to enhance collective learning within a group. This approach encourages members of a group to become aware of their individual social behavior within an environment of mutual trust. A group dynamic seminar typically begins with an unstructured format, allowing participants to experience and develop self-organization gradually. The participants must collectively determine and organize the agenda, tasks, and roles, fostering autonomy and teamwork. In the latter part of the seminar, a structured task is introduced to further enhance collaboration and problem-solving. For example, the group may be given the scenario of imagining that they are the survivors of an emergency airplane landing in the desert. They would need to work together to agree on how to prioritize a list of items from the plane, ranking them in order of importance for their survival. This exercise highlights group decision-making, negotiation, and posing diverse perspectives. At the end of the seminar, the participants share their mutual assessments of each other honestly and constructively. This process allows them to share insights about each other ' s contributions, behaviors, and interactions, fostering personal growth, trust, and improved group dynamics.

   This experience enables participants to develop greater self-awareness of their own behavior in group settings and to better understand and assess the behavior of others. They come to realize that constructive social behavior is a skill that can be learned and refined. As a result, participants gain the tools to collaborate more effectively and productively with their peers, fostering stronger partnerships and more cohesive group dynamics.

2. **Flow!**[82] Mihaly Csikszentmihalyi dedicated over two decades at the University of Chicago to researching the topic of personal feelings of happiness. By observing individuals in various professions and life situations, he conducted a study where participants were randomly contacted to describe their current state of mind. His findings revealed that people felt

happiest when they were so fully absorbed in a task that they had lost all sense of time, a state he called the phenomenon of flow. Interestingly, Csikszentmihalyi discovered that that flow is not experienced during re-laxion, such as lounging on the beach with a view of the rising or setting sun, but rather during moments of intense engagement that fully use one's own abilities. He identified clear principles that define the condi-tions for experiencing flow:

- <u>Goal-orientated activity</u>: Flow occurs when the task is directed towards achieving a specific goal. Success depends on actively choosing and pursuing a goal that is realistic for me and attaina-ble yet challenging. Regular awareness of progress toward the goal is crucial for sustaining motivation and engagement.
- <u>Clear rules for success: Flow requires clear guidelines for success and failure.</u> These rules provide structure, making it possible to measure achievement and foster a sense of accomplishment. For example, the appeal of playing chess, tennis, or mountaineering lies in mastering the established rules that apply. Without such rules, there is no benchmark for success, diminishing the sense of achievement—because there is no measure of whether the chess game or tennis match was won or lost. If you do not know the rules of successful mountaineering, you will fail on the mountain.
- <u>Optimal challenge:</u> Achieving my goal requires engaging in task that demand the best of an individual's abilities. Only when I push myself to reach the upper limit of my own capabilities can I expe-rience a feeling of joy, satisfaction, and self-affirmation associated with flow.

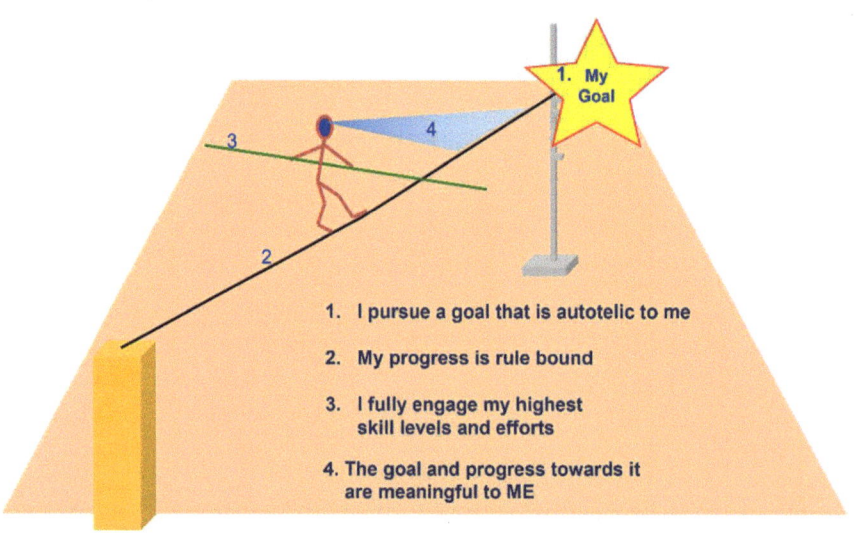

1. I pursue a goal that is autotelic to me

2. My progress is rule bound

3. I fully engage my highest skill levels and efforts

4. The goal and progress towards it are meaningful to ME

- <u>Achieving my goal is its own reward</u>. Mihaly Csikszentmihalyi described this concept as **autotelic**, derived from the Greek words *auto* (self) and *telos* (goal). An autotelic activity is one where the goal holds intrinsic value and is pursued for its own sake, not a means to an end. Vincent van Gogh did not paint to become rich; he painted just to paint—purely for the love of creating art, even though he remained poor and died in poverty.

In a state of flow, individuals become so deeply immersed in their task that they lose all sense of their surroundings, including self-awareness. In flow, time perception is profoundly altered. The sense of time is suspended: extended periods of time may seem like a fleeting moment, while brief moments may feel exceptionally long stretched. This timeless absorption, where the activity itself constitutes the quintessential value, is the hallmark of the flow experience.

3. **FlowTeam Dynamics** integrates the principles of group dynamics and flow, creating a framework that acts both as a social guard rail and a turbocharger for group productivity and creativity. This approach facilitates a form of semi-self-organization, making it particularly effective for fostering innovation.

The Swiss consultant Martin Gerber[83] introduced FlowTeam Dynamics and its foundational principles while supporting AMD in Europe. Here are six core principles:

FlowTeam Dynamics: From Individual to Group Performance

1. Commitment to teamwork: We want to achieve good teamwork and are prepared to work hard for it with dedication and effort. Good teamwork balances efficiency, having fun, and developing your talents and knowledge. Team members must be willing to invest in this process to achieve meaningful collaboration.
2. Shared goal and results: The team is driven by a shared vision and guided by a common goal and a common result that matters on multiple levels. This vision and the path to its realization are important for me, individually, for the team, for our clients, for our organization, for our society and for our environment. This common purpose provides direction and motivation for all team members.
3. Collaborative action: We act as a team. Teamwork operates according to our agreed rules of cooperation, recognizing it as both a challenge and an opportunity. Various obstacles standing in their way, such as unquestioned assumptions, unrealistic expectations, as well as unconscious positive and negative feelings and interpersonal dynamics are acknowledged and addressed to ensure effective collaboration.
4. **"Psoviem" Principle**: Produce something of value in every meeting: Every FlowTeam meeting produces concrete suggestions and tangible results that help propel the team forward. These are documented, displayed visibly on the walls of the seminar room, and compiled in paper

73

form. Individual opinions are also recorded in writing to ensure all contributions are valued.

5. Leverage individual strengths:_Each team member brings unique strengths and characteristics to the group. FlowTeams incorporate each member's individual characteristics to achieve their goals by considering even how "edgy" traits, when channeled into "the right role" can be used to advance the team's performance.

6. Visualize everything: The seminar ideally takes place in a large room (7-10 sqm per participant) without tables for the participants, with one flipchart stand per four participants. The walls should be insensitive to the use of masking tape and are used to display written flipchart pages, topic visualizations, and other paper output. This ensures that the team's growing insights, findings, and recommendations remain visible throughout the process, fostering ongoing dialogue and later presentation to clients. That is very convincing. All ideas explored. Even unconventional or crazy ideas, are retained for future consideration and potential incorporation at later stages, ensuring no valuable input is discarded.

By following these principles, FlowTeams create an environment that fosters creativity, collaboration, and tangible progress, while leveraging the unique talents and perspectives of every team member.

The Scenario Planning Extreme seminars integrate these approaches seamlessly, leveraging their unique strengths. They combine the **self-awareness and interpersonal insights** of group-dynamic, the **autotelic goal orientation** of Flow, and the **productive semi-self-organization** of FlowTeam Dynamics. This integration fosters an open-ended, creative, and collaborative environment for exploring a wide range of extreme future possibilities. Together, these methodologies empower participants to navigate uncertainty, innovate, and develop robust strategies for diverse potential scenarios.

Part II:
Scenario Planning Extreme
for Everyone

United we stand,
divided we fall.
Aesop.

10. Implement
SPX

9. Convince
Client

1. Diverse
team

8. Scenario
Alerts

2. Client
purpose

7. Scenario
Strategies

3. Key
question

6. Scenario
Storyboards

5. Imaginate
Scenarios

4. Trends

*T*he early pioneers of scenario planning were experts who developed their ideas and worked closely with decision-makers to derive implications for current decisions and craft new strategies for success.

We take a different approach. We are convinced that Scenario Planning Extreme can be equally effective when conducted by a diverse team of volunteers from all levels of the organization, complemented by interested and supportive outsiders where possible and appropriate. As described in chapter 1.6, collaborative learning within such teams can achieve a "team IQ" at a genius level, even if the individual members possess "only" average intelligence, provided they work together engaging in a constructive dialogue[84] . Because it makes the process particularly powerful, we specifically recommend this dynamic for Scenario Planning Extreme.

The process follows a clear inner logic, resembling a **journey of ten steps**. This results in a comprehensive picture of different scenarios, success strategies, plus tactical plans for implementation, equipping the organization to master the future, whatever it may look like, navigating and succeeding in any future, no matter how uncertain or extreme it may be.

Step 1: The Team

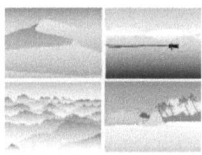

Getting together is a beginning.
Staying together is progress.
Working together is success.
Henry Ford

The principle of volunteering is fundamental for all participants in a Scenario Planning Extreme seminar. This provides a solid basis for developing self-motivation and encourages participants to take ownership of the outcomes, fostering greater later identification with the results and recommendations. To optimize the seminar's effectiveness, the group of participants should encompass as many divergent perspectives as possible on the chosen future strategies topic. The broader and more divergent the participants' viewpoints (reality tunnels), the greater the potential for discovering innovative ideas—provided, of course, that they have previously agreed on a shared goal that unites their purpose.

Drawing on insights from group dynamics, the ideal external Scenario Planning Extreme seminar team consists of approximately twenty participants. During the seminar, these participants engage with and get to know each other diverse small team assignments, allowing them to build trust and learn to complement each other's strengths. Each seminar imaginates four distinct future scenarios, brought to life by teams of five participants collaboratively addressing each scenario.

The Rules of The Seminar

1 - All in the seminar are treated equally and share the same social status, ensuring a level playing field for collaboration and idea exchange.

2 - Scenario Planning Extreme seminars embrace the motto of the Massachusetts Institute of Technology (MIT) Media Lab: *Never grow up.* As children, we are naturally open to innovative ideas, because we recognize how much we have yet to learn. We enjoy being surprised by new experiences and are eager to try out new situations and explore untested ideas. Unfortunately, this openness often diminishes as we grow up and begin to believe we know enough to succeed. The more we rely on past experiences and lessons learned from our own mistakes, the less willing we are to dare to try out new things. This hesitation becomes even more pronounced as we climb higher in the organizational ranks, where being viewed as an expert in our field can make it more difficult to open to innovative ideas outside our comfort zone or even completely beyond our experience. The explicit adoption of the mindset of *never growing up* acts as an effective antidote to this rigidity, fostering an attitude of curiosity and lifelong learning essential for innovation and growth.

3 - The deliberate choice to use "Globish", — a simplified form of global English without the pressure of strict correctness— has proved its worth as the seminar's language. This choice accommodates non-native English speakers and fosters inclusivity. Interestingly, the alienating effect of the challenge of expressing oneself in a non-native language often leads to greater clarity in articulating one's own thoughts and encourages a more meaningful and open exchange among participants.

4 – In the seminar, everyone is both a leader and a follower. Depending on the dynamics of the situation during the group's work, each participant can

seamlessly shift between both roles, being both a leader in one situation and a follower in another. The role of each participant can thus change repeatedly during the seminar. In one situation, a participant may take on the leadership role for the team when they propose the best idea for the next step toward a solution, guiding and leading the team forward. In another scenario, the same participant may step back to support and follow the great idea of another team member.

5 - <u>Learning means being imperfect.</u> This also applies to seminars. Making mistakes, learning from them quickly and improving ideas as a result increases the likelihood of successful teamwork. No one has ever learned to ride a bike without falling off it. Why should learning how to do Scenario Planning Extreme be any different? In seminars, we laugh at our mistakes and are happy when we correct them. This fluid exchange of roles fosters collaboration and ensures that the best ideas drive progress.

6 – <u>No "Yes, buts"</u>! How often do we observe in discussions where someone responds to another's argument with a "Yes, but"? This phrase is an indirect way of saying "No". As described in Chapter 1.5, the "Yes, but" approach can quickly reduce the collective intelligence level of the team, often resulting in below-average outcomes.

To address "Yes, but" habit, the agreed-upon rule in the seminars is that any „Yes, but" sentence must immediately be rephrased into a "Yes, and" format. This simple shift works remarkably well. A "Yes, and" statement signals acceptance of the other person's idea while building on it with my own. This approach fosters collaboration, quickly leading to increasingly creative cohesive concepts that everyone can identify with because everyone has jointly become co-owner. A helpful metaphor is the Union Jack, the flag of Great Britain, which combines the flags of England, Scotland, and Northern Ireland. Similarly, "Yes, and" creates a unified vision by merging diverse ideas into something greater than the sum of its parts.

7 - This goes hand in hand with the principle of <u>brainstorming</u>: all ideas are welcome, and judgment is set aside. Everyone's voice is heard, creating an environment where participants feel safe to share even seemingly unpleasant or unconventional perceptions. This openness fosters courage, enabling participants to express their thoughts freely without fear of rejection or ostracism.

8 - <u>Nora: Not one right answer.</u> Many roads lead to Rome. Encouraging the team to remain open to multiple possibilities is crucial when imagining new scenarios and strategies. The search for the "one right" scenario can paralyze teams, as

they worry and become preoccupied with avoiding the risk of missing the "best" option. Instead, the focus should be on delivering solutions that are good enough to meet the client's needs effectively.

9 - <u>Everyone is always present.</u> All team members are expected to be fully present for the entire duration of the seminar. Short-term absence due to illness or special circumstances are acceptable, provided another member temporarily steps in to fulfill the absent participant's role. Upon their return, the replacement is responsible for updating the returning member on what was missed and helping them quickly to get back on track.

10 - Does Scenario Planning Extreme also work online via <u>Zoom and Co.</u> via the Internet? Experience during the COVID-19 years suggests otherwise. Even when all seminar participants are already familiar with each other, team dynamics are significantly restricted in a virtual setting. Subtle moments of reflective hesitation, and the tactile creativity of producing wall newspapers, flipcharts, and posters for innovative concepts are all diminished or lost. While video calls can facilitate communication, they cannot fully replace the richness and effectiveness of in-person interactions.

11 - <u>Enjoy learning!</u> The basic tone of the seminar is a spirit of openness to innovative ideas and the fun of discovery, including the ability to find humor in mistakes and the creativity in fixing them. A personal story illustrates this beautifully: When Martin's teenage daughter, Susan, was hospitalized with pneumonia, Martin visited her every evening after work. What do you talk about when you cannot talk about your work? Struggling to find conversation topics unrelated to work, Susan had an idea: *"Papa, tell me a funny story."* She wanted to hear about incidents of mistakes and clumsiness that had happened to him—often only funny in hindsight. The humorous stories shared on these evening visits became a mutual delight and remain a cherished form of loving and appreciating communication to this day. Similarly with the Scenario Planning Extreme team, laughing at mistakes creates an atmosphere of quick learning and joie de vivre despite all the imperfections. Embracing imperfections along the road to success cultivates both growth and camaraderie.

12 – <u>The final rule!</u> We round off the list of rules with one that should come as no surprise: Throughout the entire seminar, <u>participants are required to set their smartphones to flight mode</u> or switch them off completely.

Be Open for New Insights

When Martin transferred from California to Geneva, his two daughters, born and raised in San Francisco, began attending the International School in Geneva. Initially, they held the strong conviction that California was the cultural center of the universe for kids. But among schoolmates from seventy different countries, they quickly learned otherwise. They realized that every culture has both its own strengths and weaknesses. They also discovered that no single culture reigns supreme. Most importantly, they discovered a universal truth: there is no universal culture, but there is a universal rule for how all people from all cultures around the world should treat each other: *First comes the person. Culture, value systems, and beliefs only follow thereafter.*

This profound insight applies to all seminar participants, serving as a guiding principle for mutual respect and collaboration.

Who are the ideal participants? Those who have demonstrated openness to change, including a willingness to challenge and test their own reality tunnels. This also includes individuals who have shown tolerance in various contexts, making them not only boundary crossers, but also future bridge builders. These participants understand how the diverse perspectives of team members can not only complement one another but also create richer and more innovative outcomes.

Consultant and author Adam Kahane[85] has spent decades mediating peace in conflict regions worldwide, including in South Africa and Colombia. In his books, Kahane shows how scenario planning can serve as an effective tool for resolving conflicts. For those interested in this topic, we highly recommend his book: *Collaborating with the Enemy. How to Work with People You Do Not Agree with or Like or Trust.*[86] Through numerous examples, Kahane describes how peace can be achieved, even between former adversaries, through open dialogue and focusing on reaching shared essential goals. He introduces the concept of "stretch collaboration", a strategy that emphasizes working together across deep divides to build sustainable solutions.

Every learning situation requires the courage to take risks, make mistakes and even run the risk of appearing foolish. Participants should embrace this courage, feeling free to express their opinions openly, even if they seem awkward in the moment. Equally important, they should remain open to ideas that run counter to their own convictions, fostering a truly dynamic and transformative learning environment.

Scenario Planning Extreme values all genuine perspectives, regardless of whether they are widely shared among the participants. In many seminars, the most interesting and relevant scenarios have emerged from trends that were initially identified by just one or two seminar participants. These unique insights often provide critical contributions to the overall process, emphasizing the importance of considering diverse viewpoints. The following perspectives reflect this principle:

- My team members are at least as complex as I am.
- I listen to them as much as I want them to listen to me.
- I put myself in their shoes and see the world through their eyes.
- I treat them the way I would like to be treated by them.

The seminar fosters an atmosphere where everyone is willing to collaborate with one another. Mutual support is integral to the process, extending to the preparation of joint presentations and the co-authored final report.

Step 2:
The Client

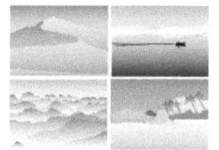

*It is granted to all people to
know themselves
and to think wisely.*
Heraclitus

W Humans are a true miracle of life. Our bodies are composed of billions of cells, most of which function autonomously yet harmoniously within our organs. These organs, too, operate independently while working in seamless coordination with each other. Books such as *The Ego Tunnel*[87] illuminate the findings of brain research, which reveal that the brain comprises different components, each with its own functions, some of which act independently, yet interconnected in complex ways. Despite this internal diversity, our self-perception is and remains holistic. To understand humanity, one must explore both our biological complexity and our self-image, hopes, and the values that guide our action. This holistic perspective is essential to comprehend and embrace what makes us who we are.

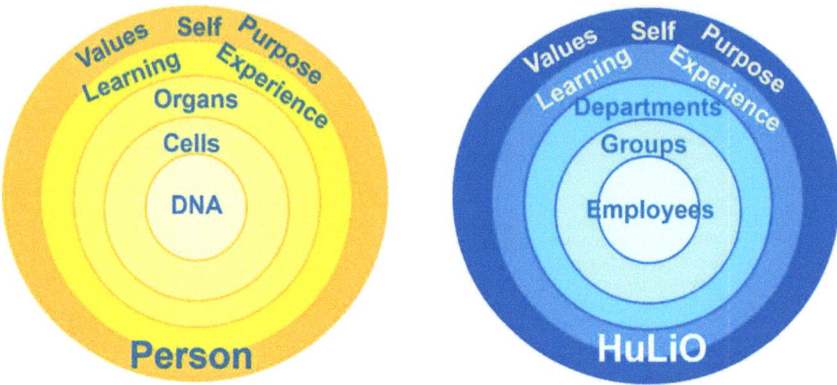

The same holistic principles that apply to individuals also apply to organizations. We follow Arie de Geus' view of seeing, understanding, and treating all organizations not only as holistic unified entities but also as analogous to human beings: human like organizations, HuLiOs[88] . In our view, organizations consist of **employees** who are organized into diverse **groups**, who in turn are combined into higher organized units—**departments**, as illustrated above. The employees in these organizations bring with them a diverse range of skills, expectations, and hopes for success and self-fulfillment. These individuals become part of the organization with its corresponding culture. Initially brought together in small organizational groups, which function as interconnected units working together within the larger organizational structure to achieve the organization's goals, these smaller organizational "bodies" are further integrated into larger systems, forming a cohesive whole at the highest level. HuLiO organizations gain new experiences daily, adapting their perspectives—reality tunnels–based on these perceptions to remain aligned with their environment and goals.

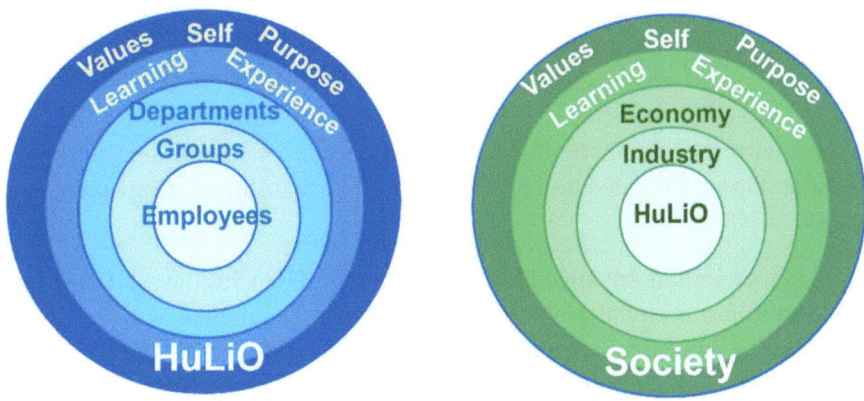

From this perspective, we see organizations as human beings—HuLiOs. Just as individuals possess a holistic self-image, organizations also understand themselves as unique entities with a comprehensive sense of identity. The accompanying illustration highlights the role of individual organizations as the foundational basis blocks upon which societies are built. It also underscores the significance of an organization's meaning and purpose within the societal framework. A society benefits from supporting the health, future viability, and sustainability of its organizations in which its citizens find meaningful work. These entities contribute to the financial foundation of societal solidarity practiced through the payment of taxes and other levies. In this way, organizations not only sustain themselves but also play a crucial role in maintaining and enhancing the well-being of the society they serve.

Why Values Are Important

When assessing which future developments are relevant for a person, it is misleading to view them merely as *homo oeconomicus*—someone who makes career choices and decisions solely to maximize personal income. A more accurate understanding emerges when we consider people in terms of their background and values.

Take Martin, for example. When asked about the meaning and purpose of his life, he answered: "*I encourage people and organizations to discover their full potential and opportunities on their own and to take full advantage of them while learning all the time."*

This perspective reflects a deeper, value-driven outlook—one that contrasts sharply with the simplistic notion of *homo oeconomicus*. Understanding values provides a more nuanced and accurate framework for predicting actions and priorities.

When Martin joined Advanced Micro Devices (AMD) in Sunnyvale, California[89], in 1980, he found an ideal environment that perfectly aligned with his self-image and values. No industry was as fast-moving and innovative as the semiconductor industry. The semiconductor industry provided the perfect backdrop for its ambitions. At AMD, the principle: *"People first. Products and profits will follow"* was not just a slogan but was reality. Years later, the company's employees further defined AMD's purpose with a clear and inspiring mission: *"We help people everywhere to lead more productive lives."* [90] This commitment to people and innovation resonated deeply with Martin and underscored the company's enduring impact.

When Martin proposed his first HR program to the AMD Executive Committee, he was met with a telling question: *"What other companies are doing the same thing?"* After listing several benchmark companies, the follow-up question came swiftly: *"If the others are doing the same thing, where is our competitive advantage?"* [91] This encapsulated AMD's ethos: to be at the forefront not only in terms of product innovation but also in terms of its groundbreaking HR programs for employees.

From that moment on, all of Martin's proposals embodied true pioneering concepts. Each subsequent concept was designed to be ahead of its time, gaining the approval of the Executive Committee and, on occasion, inspiring competitors to later copy the approach.

Scenario Planning Extreme is a testament to this same pioneering spirit of innovation. It seeks to empower all types of organizations and thus society, to become more future-ready and resilient.

The space of all possible futures is far more complex and vaster than we humans can fully grasp. So, how can we make these futures tangible? We start by first identifying which trends could become relevant for our client. We intentionally focus on the many visible trends that are already recognizable today, we narrow down the possibilities to those most aligned with, significant and relevant for the client's purpose. This approach bridges the gap between complexity and actionable insights.

The External Seminar

Experience suggests that teaching of Scenario Planning Extreme, such as at universities, is most effective in multi-day seminars. Whole-day seminars, conducted over two consecutive weekends of three days each, offer clear advantages and have proven to be an ideal format for deep engagement.

Using the European Commission as an imaginary client has proven itself to be particularly effective. The abundance of publicly available information about the EU makes it an accessible and practical case study. The seminars focus on a time horizon of 25 years, encouraging participants to think long-term.

The EU has on several occasions defined a broad array of goals and values, a veritable "flower basket" of aspirations[92] . While making an impressive list, these goals lack a clearly defined overarching purpose for the Union's existence. This ambiguity leaves open some questions about the EU's accountability in securing and improving the quality of life for its citizens.

To address this, one of the external seminar's key tasks is for participants to formulate, from their perspective, the desired enabling role of the EU in protecting and enhancing the well-being of European citizens. This exercise fosters critical thinking and creativity while addressing the challenges of shaping a purposeful future.

The In-house Seminar

On the first day of the seminar, the team focuses on defining and formulating the specific meaning, purpose, and values of their own organization. To begin, we recommend having an executive share the organization's self-image and the development of its meaning, purpose, and values in a moderated discussion. This session allows the participants to ask questions, while the seminar facilitator records the key points on flipcharts.

After the executive has departed, the participants break into small groups to refine these ideas and express the organization's purpose and values in their own words. These group formulations are then fused into a joint statement of unified merged meaning and purpose for the entire scenario team. The teams' own formulations serve as a guiding framework for the subsequent work. If the organization already has an established purpose statement that the participants already know, it can provide a solid foundation for the process so much better.

Ideally, the executive who attended the initial discussion will also join the seminar's final session, where the participants present their results. This allows the executive to gain insights into the team's strategic solutions for the identified extreme scenarios, appreciate the value of the method, and recognize the commitment and creativity of the participants.

The Pilot Project

If organizing a multi-day pilot project seminar lasting presents too great a time hurdle, a one-day pilot project is also a conceivable alternative. For this format, we suggest a group of up to twelve participants. To enhance creativity and divergence of perspectives, up to half of the participants may be selected from relevant and sympathetic outsiders, provided confidentiality concerns are addressed. Outsiders would sign a non-disclosure agreement prior to participating in the exercise.

In the run-up to the seminar, the project management team conducts interviews with the head of the organization's chosen pilot project unit, as well as the project participants. The interviews aim to clarify the purpose and values of both the organization and the unit which is participating in the pilot. Participants are also asked to identify trends they believe could become relevant.

Using the insights from the data collected from these interviews, the project management team develops a set of preliminary core findings. These findings are presented to the pilot project participants during the seminar, serving as a basis for fine tuning and building consensus.

This format offers flexibility and can be adapted in many ways. It should reflect personal sensitivities, entrepreneurial mindset, skills, and diplomacy of the pilot project's leader, as well as the organization's political context. Our advice: let prudent and diplomatic sensitivity prevail to guide the process. Often, the safest path to success is a careful and deliberate one.

A pilot project is ideally conducted in a part of the organization that is geographically distanced from its main operations. For example, in the case of AMD's marketing and sales organization, the European region proved to be the most suitable location for pilot projects, being far removed from the company's California headquarters.

Always Two Clients in Politics

In politics, there are always two clients: (a) the political organization, including its administration, and (b) the sovereign—the voters. In the first client, the procedures outlined earlier apply. However, if the focus is on the voters, it is worth clarifying in advance how they will be involved in the process. This ensures that they can engage with the project and gradually identify with its goals and outcomes—step by step.

Step 3:
The Key Question

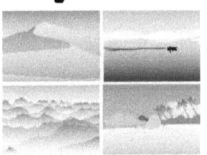

*Questions are more important
than answers.*
Immanuel Kant

I n a Scenario Planning Extreme project, the focus is always centered on a specific, strategically significant question for the organization. This approach narrows the otherwise vast array and unlimited possibilities of potential future scenarios, enabling the seminar team to focus their efforts effectively and maintain a clear direction in their work.

Here are three from seminars conducted with the EU Commission as a simulated client, focusing on Europe 25 years into the future:

- The EU and the future of individual mobility: Exploring the evolution of transportation systems, infrastructure, and policies to ensure sustainable, efficient, and inclusive mobility across Europe.

- The EU and large-scale migration from North Africa and the Middle East: Addressing the challenges and opportunities associated with demographic shifts, migration patterns, and the integration of diverse populations within the EU framework.

- The EU, AI, and the future of individual work: Investigating the impact of artificial intelligence on employment, workforce dynamics, and the broader implications for labor policies and societal well-being.

These scenarios highlight critical strategic considerations for the EU as it navigates complex challenges and opportunities in a rapidly changing global environment.

Before the seminar begins, participants collaborate in groups of three to identify key trends relevant to the given seminar topic. Each group then creates a movie poster depicting a world shaped by these trends. These posters are then presented and explained at the beginning of the seminar, setting the stage for deeper exploration and discussion of the scenarios envisioned.

Prepared to address the client's key issues in this way, participants work in small groups to suggest their own wordings for the key question, guided by the agreed upon definition of the client's purpose. The various proposed wordings are then compared and refined. Finally, the entire seminar team votes on a unified formulation that serves as the foundation to frame the subsequent scenario development. The following are examples of key questions formulated in seminars for the three topics previously mentioned above:

- **The EU and the Future of Individual Mobility**: How can the EU promote more socially, economically, and ecologically sustainable, inclusive, and innovative mobility across Europe over the next 25 years?

- **The EU and large-scale migration from North Africa and the Middle East**: How can the EU optimize the benefits of diversification to address and integrate large-scale migration while strengthening security, harmony, and prosperity in a sustainable, socially cohesive, and economically stable way?
- **The EU, AI, and the future of individual work:** How can the EU prepare for the transformative impact of AI on employment, ensuring equitable opportunities and workforce adaptability, thereby limiting the potential disadvantages of AI to ensure a meaningful and economically appropriate life, while simultaneously harnessing AI's positive societal impact?

These examples show how the process of clarifying the key strategic question not only strengthens a sense of co-ownership among the team members and helps to narrow down the search focus for possible extreme scenarios. By establishing agreed content guidelines, the teams are better equipped to later develop organization-relevant and actionable success strategies.

With this foundation in place as an introduction, the scenario teams are well-prepared to explore and consider various possibilities for the future.

Step 4:
Relevant Trends

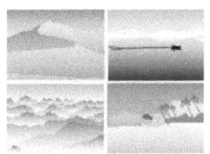

Attentiveness is life!
Johann Wolfgang von Goethe

*S*cenario Planning Extreme continues with the identification and compilation of all trends that could influence the strategic issue. These trends serve as the building blocks for constructing future scenarios. The process of searching for these trends is critical, as it forms the foundation for every Scenario Planning Extreme project, enabling comprehensive exploration to identify potential future developments.

In this step, we are interested in identifying all current trends, regardless of their scale or nature. These trends may be major or minor, and they can be perceived as favorable, unfavorable, pleasant, unpleasant, or even threatening from our point of view. All trends are considered equally important and interesting because the future does not care about our views, unfolding independently of our personal wishes, desires, or convictions. By embracing this unbiased approach, we ensure a comprehensive and open-minded exploration of possibilities for the project.

When identifying trends, we are interested in quantity and inclusivity, welcoming all points of view, including deliberately divergent individual observations. Equally important is promoting a team atmosphere where even uncomfortable suggestions are heard and valued. This openness contributes to a more encompassing perception of the whole, fostering a comprehensive understanding of the broader picture. The usefulness of this approach stems from the diversity of the trends identified, and the seminar's rules encourage and support this divergence to enrich the process.

The ideal scenario team is composed of members who embody courage, openness, and curiosity. Do you dare to share a trend that challenges established perceptions of reality when you see a trend that runs counter to current reality maps? Are you open to listening when an observation that runs counter to your convictions? Do you possess the curiosity to explore added information and think about its broader implications?

History reminds us of the risks associated with presenting ideas that defy prevailing beliefs. Galileo Galilei immediately comes to mind. He faced severe consequences for his scientific discoveries, contradicting the dominant worldview of his time. Similarly, Charles Darwin hesitated for many years before publishing *On the Origin of Species* in 1859, anticipating the controversy his book would ignite. Fortunately, while Darwin avoided the fate that befell Galileo, both men demonstrated immense courage in sharing their groundbreaking insights with us. In the face of real risks to life and liberty, their bravery not only advanced human knowledge but also serves as a testament to the value of questioning and expanding our understanding of the world.

While the risks of sharing controversial observations are different today, they can still be risky, nonetheless. The success of Scenario Planning Extreme relies heavily on the courage of its members to share their views with the team members. They depend on the openness of the team to consider unconventional or controversial observations, as well as their collective curiosity to explore the potential implications of these ideas. To foster this safe and trusting environment the "Las Vegas agreement" applies to all team members: *"What happens in a scenario team stays in the scenario team, except for what we agree to make part of our scenarios."* This principle ensures that participants feel secure in sharing their insights without fear of judgment or external repercussions, encouraging the free flow of ideas essential for the process.

Preparation for the Seminar

Participants are introduced to the specific content of the Scenario Planning Extreme seminar through a pre-seminar announcement. This announcement outlines the seminar's focus and objectives, ensuring that participants are adequately informed. They are encouraged to familiarize themselves with the topic in advance, identify some relevant trends from their point of view, and bring along their notes on these trends to the seminar. This preparation equips participants to contribute meaningfully to the discussions and enhances the effectiveness of the scenario development process.

During the Seminar

During the seminar, the principle of brainstorming is applied during the search for trends, emphasizing inclusivity and creativity: all ideas are welcome, and all participant's observations are taken on board. At this stage, quantity takes precedence over quality to ensure a broad spectrum of perspectives is captured.

The focus is on identifying all trends relevant to the key question, particularly those emerging from the world of various stakeholders. These interest groups are important to the organization. These stakeholders include interest groups who can influence the organization's clients, including suppliers, investors, and supervisory authorities, as well as relevant trade unions, lobbyists, and non-governmental organizations. Depending on the key question, these groups can all significantly impact the organization, by supporting, hindering, promoting, or opposing its goals. Recognizing the potential roles of these stakeholders ensures a comprehensive and well-rounded exploration of trends that matter.

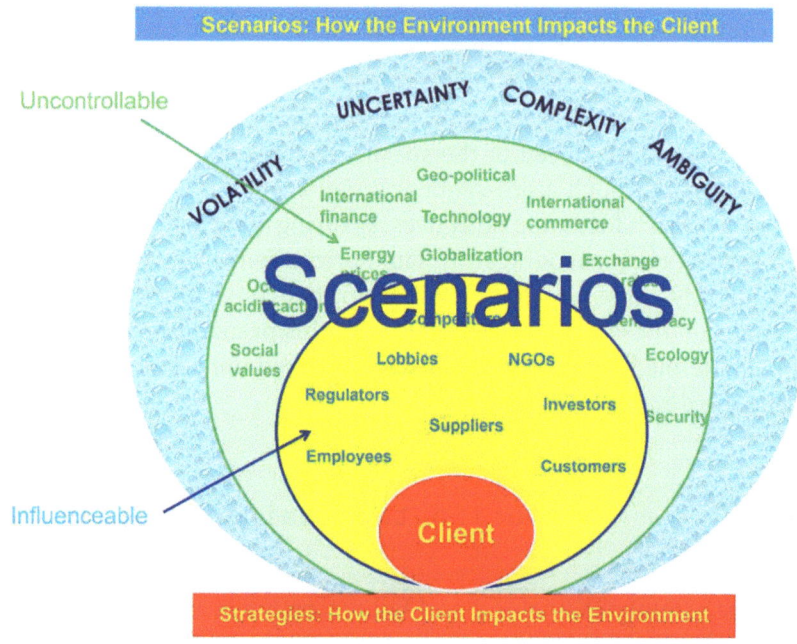

We are also interested in relevant trends that lie beyond the world of stakeholders: including the environment, State policies, globalization, energy markets, international finance, security, and social norms. These trends typically fall into five distinct categories: politics, economics, environment, social values, and technology.

In their search for trends, participants often confuse trends with strategies. Trends shape the organization's future, acting as the subject, while the organization is the object influenced by these external forces. Conversely, the organization responds as subject by developing strategies to influence the environment as the object, as our illustration shows. While trends and strategies are often intertwined, Scenario Planning Extreme clearly separates them with a simple guiding question: *Who is acting on whom?* Trends act on the organization, and strategies act on the trends. Initial ideas for strategies, however, are set aside in Step 4 and revisited during the strategy development phase in Step 7.

From Individual Observations to a Unified Trend Wall

Dialogue within groups works best when their size ranges between three to five participants. That is why we start with several small groups where individual members contribute and share their ideas collaboratively. Together, they compile lists of trends, organizing them on a separate flipchart for each group and sorting them into opportunities and threats. These flipchart lists are then displayed on the seminar walls using adhesive tape, presented in a plenary session, and explained. This process includes a Q&A segment, allowing all participants to familiarize themselves with and understand the full spectrum of all the identified trends.

Each participant then selects and writes down the seven to twelve trends they personally consider most relevant to the strategic issue on individual post-its notes (ideal size 76 x 127 mm). These trends may come from one of the flip chart discussions or reflect new observations that were not previously mentioned. With twenty participants, this process can produce up to two hundred cards. All the cards are then collected and displayed together on a common trend wall, creating a shared visual representation of the group's collective insights.

Before contributing to the common trend wall, each participant pairs up with a partner to mutually check each other's post-its notes for consistency with the agreed-upon format for trends. Each trend should be succinctly summarized with a short, clear headline describing the trend, such as *"The number of e-bikes in cities is increasing significantly."* During this dialogue, any strategies identified are separated and laid aside for consideration in a later phase, ensuring the focus remains solely on trends at this stage.

The entire seminar team then gathers in front of the shared trend wall (typically six flipchart sheets taped together) to begin organizing the trends. The process starts with a single Post-it note, which is attached to the trend wall. The corresponding trend Post-it notes with similar content from other members are then added and grouped together, forming the first trend group. Once participants understand the trend sorting process, they self-organize all the remaining trends into trend groups of varying sizes. Some trends are named by many groups; other trend groups can be smaller and may even consist of only one item. During this trend sorting process, the team can continuously adjust the assignments of individual trends to different groups as needed. This flexibility is the reason Post-it notes are used, allowing for easy reorganization as new patterns and corrections emerge.

From individually perceived trends to joint trend wall

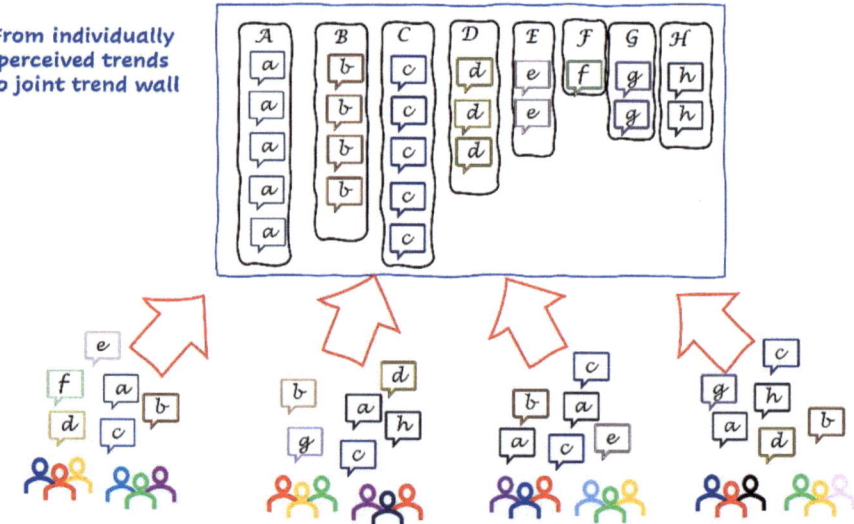

At the end of the sorting process, participants engage in a fun and creative task: the participants find a suitable nickname for each trend group. Good nicknames have a high recall value, succinctly capturing the essence of the trend group, getting to the heart of the meaning, and using humor to make them distinctive, recognizable, memorable, and easy to communicate. Adding humorous nicknames also helps to alleviate any anxiety associated with more daunting or threatening trend groups, as this illustration shows[93]. This lighthearted activity fosters team engagement and ensures the trends are more approachable.

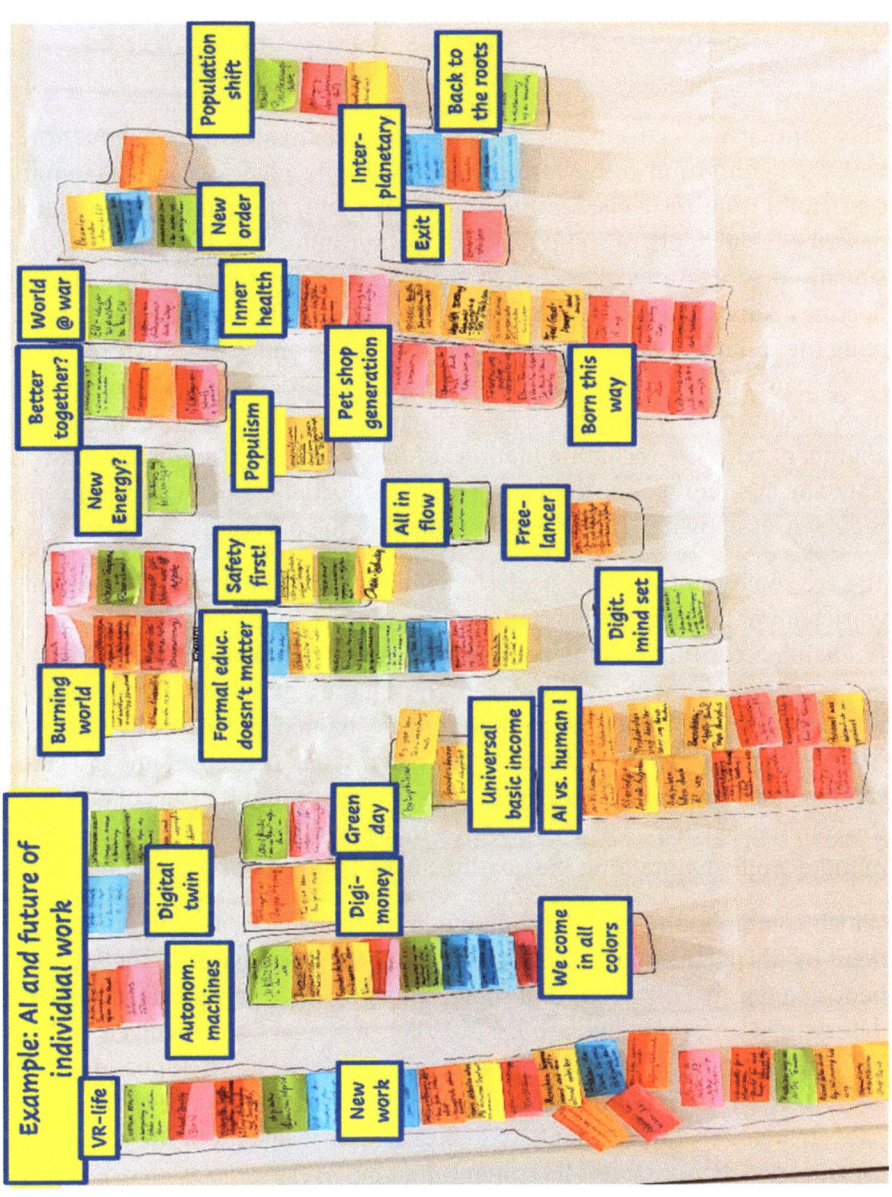

Co-Ownership Versus Time Constraints

This approach effectively engages seminar participants, fostering identification with the method and empowering them to become advocates for its later application. But it requires considerable time investment, often taking several hours as described. The depth of trend research further influences the time needed. Occasionally, organizations allocate less than six days for an initial trial seminar, reflecting an understandable desire to save time. Nonetheless, shortcuts when creating the trend wall should be avoided. The active and visible involvement of the participants in the trend search and clustering process is crucial for achieving high-quality results and ensuring subsequent participation identification and alignment with the recommendations of the Scenario Planning Extreme project. Allowing members to see their perceptions reflected in the outcomes strengthens their senses of ownership and commitment to the process.

To save some seminar time, project facilitators can undertake some preparatory work before the seminar. This involves meeting individually with participants beforehand, recording their perceived trends and compiling these insights into a preliminary version of the trend wall. During the seminar, this preliminary trend wall can be supplemented, expanded, and nicknamed by the participants. In other words, the less time allocated for the seminar itself, the more time must be dedicated to conducting preliminary discussions between the project facilitators and the seminar participants. This ensures that participants' perspectives are incorporated while maintaining the quality and engagement of the seminar process.

Which combination of preparation by the seminar facilitators and time commitment by the participants makes the most sense? The answer to that question depends on the specific needs and constraints of each organization and can only be determined on a case-by-case basis. When managers are involved, holding the seminar as a "learning conference" over a weekend at an appealing venue has proven effective. This approach offers fair compensation for the willingness of the management level participants to dedicate their weekend to the topic, while the organization demonstrates its commitment by covering the associated costs. Such an arrangement not only fosters engagement but also creates a conducive environment for deep learning and collaboration.

Step 5:
From Trends to Extreme Scenarios

Imagination is more important
than knowledge.
Albert Einstein

*I*n front of the common trend wall, the seminar team now imaginates a scenario where each of these trends grows exponentially over the next 25 years, significantly influencing the strategic question. They envision a world where these developments could lead to fundamental change for the organization, with extreme consequences for its processes, products, services, and strategies.

With such exponential changes in mind, the seminar team then identifies the ten most concerning or frightening trends related to the key question and documents them on a separate flipchart. The seminar facilitator helps the team to focus not solely on the most "popular" trends that were perceived by many participants from the trend wall but also ensures that attention is given to the smaller trends, which also deserve equal attention in this selection process, as they may hold significant implications for the organization despite their lower visibility.

From this list of the ten <u>most frightening trends,</u> the team narrows their focus to the five trends that represent the <u>greatest uncertainties</u> for the key question. In the last step, the team then chooses the two core trends from these five most uncertain trends, which, in their view, they believe are the <u>most relevant and impactful</u> in shaping potential answers to the key question[94]. This structured process ensures that both major and nuanced influences are considered in building robust scenarios.

It is essential that the two core trends should be <u>orthogonal</u>–<u>independent of each other</u> in terms of content—to ensure a robust framework for scenario development. These two chosen exponential core trends become the dominant forces shaping four distinct scenarios based on the following logic: since the direction of their change cannot be predicted, each trend is imagined in a positive and a negative trend trajectory. This approach results in a 2x2 matrix with four cells, each representing a unique scenario based on the interaction of the two trends in their respective directions.

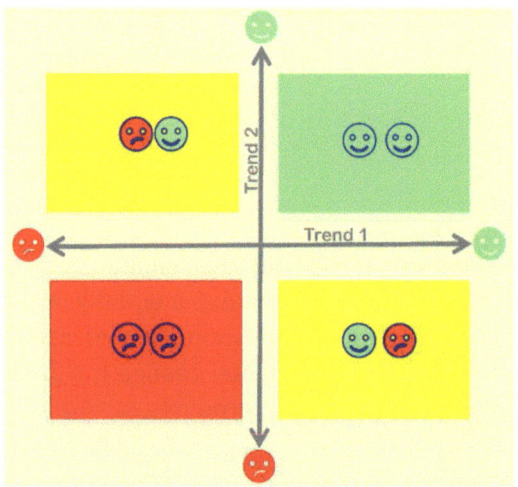

In one of the four scenarios, both **positive versions** of the two core trends shape the narrative, creating an optimistic outlook. In another scenario, the **negative sides** of both trends dominate, portraying a more challenging or adverse future. The third and fourth scenarios are defined by **mixed outcomes**, where the positive effects of one core trend interact with the negative effects of the other. Our experience shows that the most interesting and relevant scenarios often arise from the combination of a trend that was widely recognized by many team members and a second trend that is more **controversial** for the client. Such controversial trends are often suggested during the trend-sorting process by just a few courageous members, bringing unique and thought-provoking perspectives to the discussion.

Next, the team works in four small groups to develop suggestions for memorable **movie titles** that capture the essence of each scenario. These titles are then presented and discussed in a plenary session, where the members vote on the most suitable titles. To ensure fairness, participants are not allowed to vote for the suggestions proposed by their own smaller group. The chosen titles should provide a vivid and engaging glimpse into what life might look like in each scenario.

Here are three examples of movie titles from the three Scenario Planning Extreme seminar topics described above. From the seminar "Europe and the Future of Individual Mobility", the team chose the following trends for defining the scenarios: data security and the trend towards the metropolization of society. The resulting movie titles offer a creative foretaste of the scenarios shaped by these trends highlighting a preview of what life will look like in them.

The seminar addressing "Mass immigration from North Africa and the Middle East to Europe in 2016", developed the following scenarios. Chapter 3.2 includes an article written by the students of this seminar, which was published in 2016 in the journal *Acamonta* of the TU Bergakademie Freiberg.

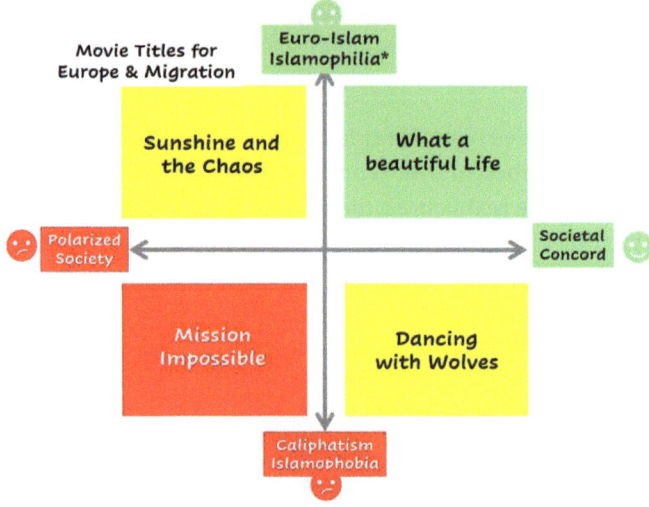

*A perspective characterized by a harmonious integration of Islam within European societies, with mutual respect, appreciation, and positive engagement between European and Islamic cultures.

The third example of scenarios explores "Europe and the Future of AI". Here too, the scenario titles provide a glimpse into what various extreme futures might entail.

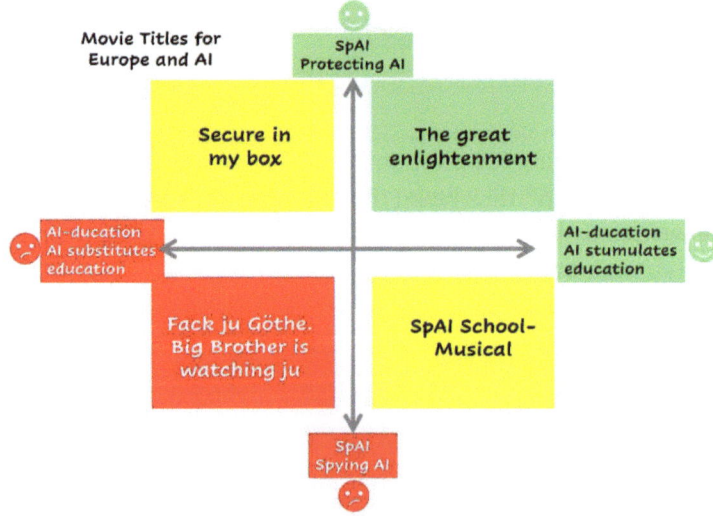

Nicknames for trend groups can achieve remarkably high recognition value among the team members, as they evoke memories of the seminar discussions. At the same time, however, they may require additional explanation for those outside the group. This is particularly evident in the above-mentioned word hybrids created from the two core trends. For example, SpAI combines *spying* and *artificial intelligence* (*AI*). AI-ducation merges the terms *AI* and *education*. These creative nicknames capture the essence of the trends while also reflecting the discussions that shaped them.

Step 6:
Storyboards

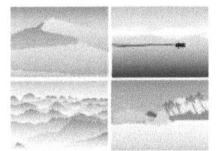

As you go the way of life,
you will see a great chasm.
Jump!
It is not as wide as you think.
Native American proverb [95]

I f the purpose of extreme scenario planning is to help an organization—and, by extension, society—to maintain and enhance their future viability, identifying the relevant trends is essential, as they provide the foundation for learning and drawing the right conclusions. But how do we learn effectively?

Johann Heinrich Pestalozzi, a pioneer of universal education, emphasized that genuine and lasting learning engages the **head**, **heart**, and **hand**: understanding, valuing/appreciating, and practicing. Interestingly, the Native American traditions embraced this integrated approach long before Pestalozzi's time. Their wisdom highlights that true learning often begins with the heart, as their proverb states: *We can only learn when our heart is ready*. This insight underscores the importance of emotional readiness as the starting point for meaningful learning and growth.

Why is this important? Let us remember that our individual respective reality tunnels and our meanings of life are deeply intertwined, much like Siamese Twins. Fascinating and vivid scenarios enable us to make mental leaps over deep

109

emotional abysses in a playful and imaginative fashion before taking real-world action by physically jumping across the chasm. Through these scenarios, we can visit different possible futures, immerse ourselves in them, move around in them, and try out our existing recipes for success within these unfamiliar worlds. We can thus recognize how they would prove themselves in the new imagined possibilities. If our current approaches do not work in these simulated environments, it is not a disaster, after all, it is only a simulation. Instead, it offers a valuable opportunity to experiment by having a playful look around and exploring alternatives to our current recipes for success in a safe, creative space. This process allows us to identify and refine strategies that might succeed in these new contexts, setting the stage for the strategy development we outline in the next chapter.

Fascinating and convincing scenarios provide powerful tools and wonderful ways for orientating ourselves in new and evolving, constantly changing worlds. They help us to understand them, to recognize their potential benefits (for ourselves and others), and to make informed decisions to prepare for and leverage them to our advantage.

How do I breathe life into my scenarios? By using a technique that has long been used in the film industry: **Storyboards**, visualize all scenes before filming begins, bringing ideas to life through structured, visual storytelling. This method was famously utilized by Sergei Eisenstein as early as 1925 for the iconic silent film *Battleship Potemkin*[96] . Today, storyboards remain a cornerstone of filmmaking, from adventure blockbusters, such as the George Lucas movies *Star Wars* in the 1970s[97] to postmodern productions, such as Wes Anderson's *Asteroid City*[98] in 2023. Similarly, storyboards can transform abstract scenarios into vivid and relatable narratives, enhancing their impact and clarity.

We adapt the concept of storyboards to develop our various extreme scenarios by imagining the scenario worlds step by step in the team, a process we will explore in a moment. This approach provides the team members with both the freedom to unleash their imagination and the structure of content guidelines to ensure coherence and focus.

After defining the themes and movie titles for the four scenarios, in **Step 5**, we move to **Step 6**, where we bring the scenarios to life. The four scenarios are developed simultaneously in parallel by four separate groups. Seminar participants are invited to volunteer for the scenario they are most interested in working on. If the distribution is uneven, we first ask for volunteers who are willing to switch to one of the "understaffed" scenarios. Should this does not reach the desired near-equal staffing distribution for each scenario, we use a coin flip to finalize the group assignments. This ensures balanced team sizes for effective collaboration.

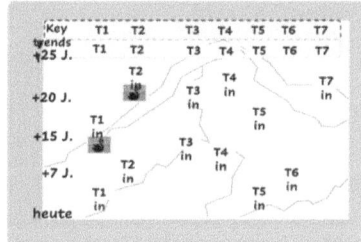

Each team imaginates its assigned scenario in detail. A well-developed scenario should meet the following criteria:

- **Possible**: Even if it seems unlikely from today's perspective, the scenario must remain within the realm of possibility
- **Plausible and internally consistent**: The scenario's elements should logically fit together and adhere to a consistent internal narrative.
- **Relevant**: The scenario must address the client's key question directly and meaningfully.
- **Easy to understand and highly memorable**: The scenario should be straightforward, engaging, and leave a lasting impression.

- **Challenges current conventions:** The scenario should call into question existing norms and assumptions, highlighting potential shifts in rules of the game.

These five attributes ensure that scenarios are robust, thought-provoking, and valuable for strategic exploration.

The storyboard for each scenario is created on a Scenario Story Board created by taping together four flipchart sheets with masking tape. The first step is to draw a silhouette of a mountain, symbolizing the ascent to the imagined Scenario Mountain Top, which represents the scenario as envisioned in the target year— 25 years into the future.

This metaphor connects with the mountain and skiing imagery introduced earlier in the book: We first imagine the Scenario Mountain at its peak, visualizing the future state. From there, we then elegantly "ski down" the mountain with innovative back casting strategies, a process that we will describe in greater detail in the next chapter. This approach combines creativity and structure, guiding participants to envision the future and plan steps to navigate toward it.

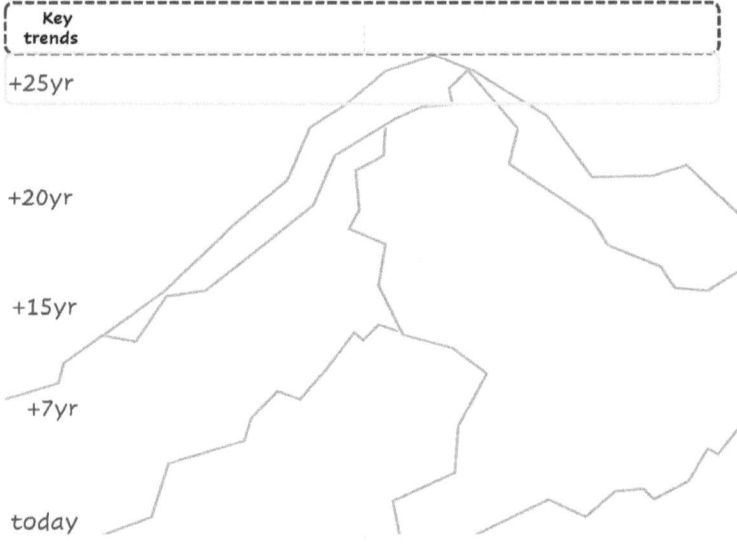

The left-hand column shows the 25-year timeline, with the present at the bottom and the envisioned future that awaits us, at the top. The **top row** will name the seven trends which will make up the storyline of the scenario. The two leftmost trends are the two key trends that set the tone for the scenario. The **second row** describe on cards what each of these seven trends will look like in 25 years. An extended headline for each trend will suffice. This structured layout ensures clarity and coherence, allowing participants to visualize the evolution of trends and their impact on the scenario over time.

It has worked well in practice that the scenario teams begin with the two key trends for their scenario and their directions (positive or negative), and imaginate what that trend combination will look like in 25 years. They also imaginate **two black swan events**–unpredictable, high-impact occurrences– that explain how and when the two core trends have changed exponentially. These events give plausibility to the scenario's trajectory.

To enrich their scenario with vivid details, each team chooses five additional trend groups from the trend wall that fit, expand, and complement their scenario. These trend groups are added to their storyboard on cards, following the same format as the two core trends. Additionally, each team includes **five cards** that describe how the selected five additional trend groups will look like in 25 years. Each card features a short, concise headline summarizing the future state of these trends. This step adds depth and richness to the scenario, ensuring that the supporting trends are clearly defined and aligned with the imagined future. This process ensures the scenarios are detailed, diverse and deeply engaging.

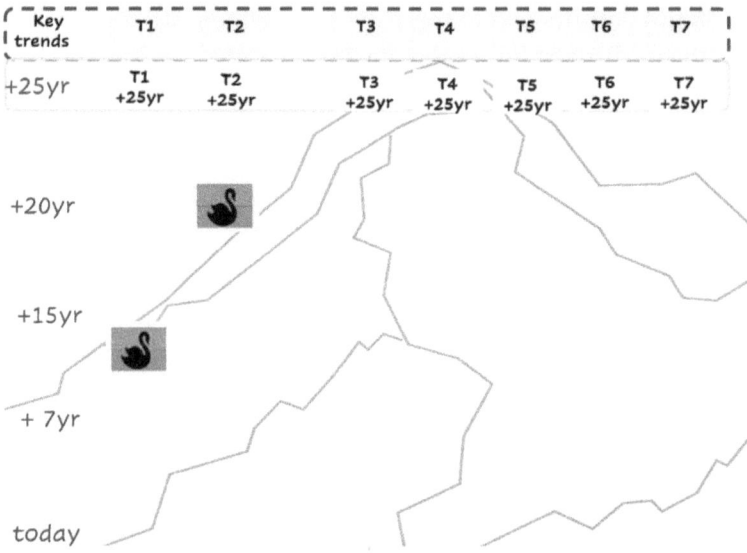

Key trends	T1	T2		T3	T4	T5	T6	T7
+25yr	T1 +25yr	T2 +25yr		T3 +25yr	T4 +25yr	T5 +25yr	T6 +25yr	T7 +25yr
+20yr								
+15yr								
+ 7yr								
today								

Now that the scenario team has outlined its initial take on the future world for its scenario, it is time to check it for consistency through partner review. Each scenario team member pairs up with someone from another scenario team. In this exchange, one member explains the logic of their scenario, including the seven trends, two Black Swan events, and a description of what the scenario world will look like in the target year. This cross-scenario discussion provides valuable feedback, encourages fresh perspectives, and helps refine the consistency and plausibility of the scenarios.

The partner provides feedback by highlighting aspects that seem logical, noting any surprising elements, and identifying components they can clearly recognize and relate to very well. If they have specific suggestions for improving the scenario's clarity or coherence, they share those ideas as well. After this exchange, the partners swap roles, and the process is repeated to discuss their partner's scenario.

Once the feedback session is complete, each scenario team member then returns to their team. Together, they incorporate the feedback from their various partners, refining their own scenario to make it more compelling, clear, and convincing. This collaborative process improves the overall quality and consistency of the scenarios.

Now that the worlds of the various scenarios have become more clearly defined, recognizable, and comprehensible, the teams begin the process of back casting—imaginating, with hindsight from the target year, how these future scenarios came to be. This involves working backward from the envisioned future to the current year in a series of logical steps.

Each scenario team imaginates the most important and interesting developments of the trends between the targeted future and today. These developments are documented on cards, using short and vivid headlines that make them clear and imaginable. These cards are then attached to the Scenario Story Board, creating a visual timeline of key milestones. Ten to twelve well-chosen examples will suffice to illustrate the pathway from the present to the imaginated future.

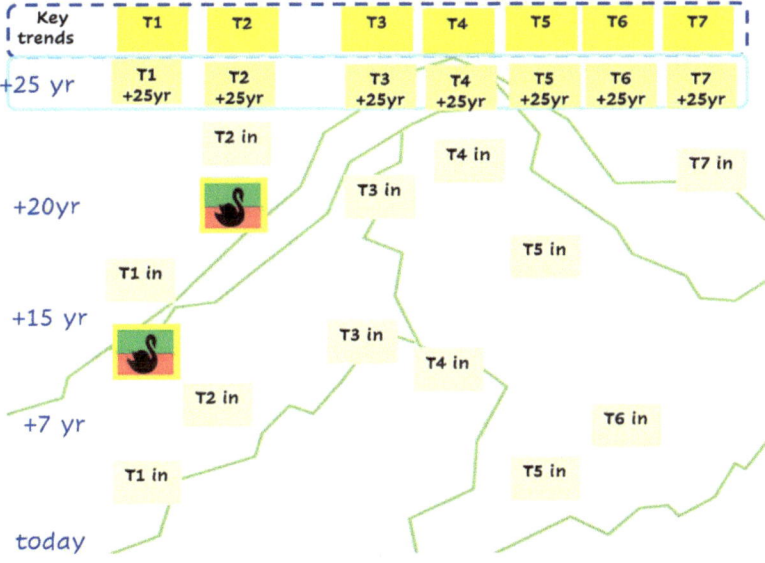

These examples of specific trend developments are invaluable later for linking the present with the future scenario, adding credibility to the scenario's plausibility, even when it appears unlikely from today's perspective. By illustrating logical progression, they help ground the scenario in realistic developments, making it more convincing.

This task is again followed by a round of mutual consultations with a partner from another team, following the same procedure as described earlier. Each partner reviews the developments, provides feedback on their logic and coherence, and suggests improvements to enhance clarity and plausibility. This iterative process ensures that each scenario becomes more robust and compelling.

Scenarios as Personas

With all the essential elements of the scenarios now assembled, the next step is to bring them to life as cohesive, vivid personas. Metaphorically speaking, all the "body parts" of the scenario are in place, and the scenario just needs to be animated with a personality and character. The easiest and most effective way to achieve this is by creating a captivating movie poster.

Our experience shows that ideally allowing some time interval between constructing the scenario and creating the corresponding poster is beneficial. Just as we can better recognize a mountain from a distance, participants gain clarity and perspective from temporal distance. During their time off from scenario imaginating, the participants are likely to continue to reflect on their scenarios. They may even discover innovative ideas they did not initially consider when first creating the scenario.

Each team works together to design and hand-draw the poster, bringing their scenario's world to life through their collective perspective. A great poster is

- Captivating, drawing immediate interest.
- Memorable, leaving a lasting impression.
- Immersive, depicting how people would live and feel in the extreme futures imagined.

Why should the posters be hand-drawn? It strengthens identification and motivation among team members. It also enables a tangible link between the scenario and the concrete people who created it. As Martin Gerber from FlowTeam Dynamics repeatedly pointed out[99] a hand-drawn poster is a shared creation that reflects the collective effort, joint result, and the identity of the people who created the scenario. The team recognizes itself in the poster, which becomes a symbol of their joint success.

Unlike polished, computer-generated compositions, a hand-drawn poster is a thousand times more authentic and convincing. It demonstrates to the client that the scenario was developed by real people who deeply identify with it. This personal connection fosters trust and credibility—just as we are most likely to follow the advice of a friend we trust.

The same applies to photo reproductions of flipcharts from a seminar. These visual reminders resonate with participants because they reflect what they have created themselves, fostering a sense of ownership and connection. In contrast, write-ups of flip charts on standard documents lose identity and all personal traces to the people who created them. No wonder that most of them are often quickly discarded and forgotten along with the pearls of insight from the meeting.

Martin Gerber advised his clients to transform the original flipcharts into postcard-sized booklets and distribute them to participants and the client representatives. He was right. It worked for Martin and the teams he worked with. These postcard sized booklets are easy to carry as a pocketbook, and are accessible, tangible references for future brainstorming.

Step 7: Strategies

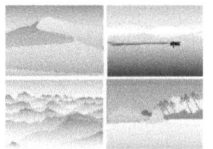

It is not because it is difficult that we do not dare to do it,
but because we do not dare to do it that it is difficult.
Seneca

*T*he previous steps of the Scenario Planning Extreme project were preparations for the development of strategies that will help the organization to remain successful in a rapidly changing world. Now is the time for answers and solutions.

The development of strategies is based on the characteristics of their respective scenarios. We ask ourselves what the key opportunities and risks are for the client in each specific scenario world. How can we exploit the opportunities? How can we minimize the negative effects of these risks for the client? What positive results do we want to achieve? What do we want to have realized in the target year of the scenario, i.e., today plus 25 years?

Transform or Adapt!

Martin's father repeatedly gave him advice that goes back to the German American theologian Reinhold Niebuhr[100] : "*Whenever you are angry about something, ask yourself whether you can change it. If so, do not get angry. Change it. If you cannot change it, do not get angry. Instead, make the best of it. May you develop the wisdom to distinguish one from the other.*"[101] Niebuhr described the first situation as transformative, the second as adaptive.

Applied to the core threats and core opportunities of a scenario, this results in a two-by-two matrix for strategic approaches.

	Scenario Characteristics	
	Key Downsides	**Key Upsides**
1. Transform if you can change it	**Build dikes against rising sea**	**See new opportunity?** **Be Steve Jobs**
2. Adapt if you can't	**Got only lemons?** **Make Lemonade**	**Surf is up?** **Go surfing**

Strategy Options

Transformative strategies enable us to influence and change the world based on its opportunities and risks. A historical example of a transformative strategy against a major threat are the dikes in the Netherlands, which were constructed by the Dutch to reclaim land from the sea. Steve Jobs was known for recognizing new opportunities and taking advantage of them with transformative strategies before others did.

Adaptive strategies are characterized by the saying: When life gives you lemons, make lemonade. The same applies to adaptive strategies for opportunities. They are like waves that come at us. We can adapt to them and surf them.

Let us look at some examples:

		Scenario Characteristics	
		Key Downsides	Key Upsides
Strategy Options	1. Transform if you can change it	Biontech GMO vaccines fight against COVID	Steve Jobs transforms phones into smartphones
	2. Adapt if you can't	3M Turn Goldmine desaster into innovations	Google Android rides the iPhone wave

The company BioNTech[102] has succeeded in combating the threat of the coronavirus in a revolutionary way. Their groundbreaking mRNA vaccine technology helped the world to contain the impact of the deadly virus. This benefited not only the company, but also humanity.

Steve Jobs changed our world with his iPhones. He was the first to recognize and use the possibilities of transforming Apple's iPod MP3 music device into a smartphone, which changed our world of communication including his invention of social media.

When it comes to adaptive strategies for dealing with key threats, the 3M Corporation (Minnesota Mining and Manufacturing)[103] immediately comes to mind. 3M was founded by three brothers who bought a gold mine in the State of Minnesota, but found no gold in it, just sand, brittle, hard stones, and lots of it. Give up? The brothers recognized the properties of the brittle stones - and invented sandpaper instead.

How can you deal with a core opportunity that is already being used by someone else, e.g., the iPhone? Google bought the Android Operating System and Samsung corporation was the first to imitate the iPhone device to the point of infringing Apple's patent rights. Both have profited from the iPhone transformation.

How can the world of politics deal with its major opportunities and risks, and address it with transformative and adaptive strategies?

When the EU Commission is used as an imaginary client in our external Scenario Planning Extreme seminars, we take a closer look at some examples from politics. Politicians achieve their goals indirectly by influencing companies and citizens, by encouraging or discouraging them to act in the strategic interest of politics. It was not for nothing that former German Chancellor Helmut Schmidt pointed out in an interview[104] that on the federal government level in Germany, economic policy is made not by the Ministry of Economic Affairs but by the Ministry of Finance: through tax legislation and financial incentives.

Government empowers pioneers		Scenario Characteristics	
		Key Downsides	Key Upsides
	1. Transform — if you can change it	Change the rules of the game	Identify future champions
	2. Adapt — if you can't	Incentivize next gen innovation	Attract world champions

Core opportunities influence policy by identifying potential pioneers and encouraging them. Where adaptation is appropriate, government action fosters economic growth through targeted promotion of innovation in future technologies. If companies in other countries are far ahead of their own industry, they can be encouraged through financial incentives to also open production facilities in the politicians' own country, a strategy that the State of Singapore has pursued for 50 years with outstanding results.

		Scenario Characteristics	
		Key Downsides	Key Upsides
Government empowers pioneers	1. Transform if you can change it	Norway stepwise phase-out of gasoline cars	DARPA Trigger autonomous driving through contests
	2. Adapt if you can't	SEMATECH Matches US SCI cooperative research investments	Saxony attract SIEMENS, AMD & create Silicon Saxony industry cluster

Let us take the worldwide threat of climate change. The EU has concluded that it must learn to live without combustion engines. Norway was the first European country to take the path of gradually banning cars with combustion engines.

The US Defense Advanced Research Projects Agency (DARPA)[105] sees itself as a pioneer in the identification and promotion of innovative technologies that could be decisive in a war. The innovations in question usually have „dual use", i.e., both military and civilian use. At the beginning of this century, DARPA recognized the potential military utility of autonomous vehicles and held a competition for autonomous driving in open terrain. The prize was a mere $1 million. No vehicle made it in the first year. So, DARPA doubled the reward to $2 million and repeated it the following year. At that time, a VW SUV with a navigation and orientation system designed by Stanford University researchers won. In subsequent years, DARPA organized annual competitions for autonomous driving in road traffic. With growing success: in 2023, a dozen US cities gave autonomous cabs permission to drive on their streets[106].

An example of a government responding to key threats over which it has no control is the US government's fifty percent co-funding of the US semiconductor industry research cooperative SEMATECH. [107]

It can be worthwhile for countries to use financial incentives to try and attract the best global companies to their own country. In 2023, the German government convinced Intel to build a factory operated with projected 10,000 jobs in Magdeburg with a €10 billion subsidy[108]. Unfortunately, this investment was withdrawn within a few months after its announcement. The US government did something similar when it convinced world chip foundry champion Taiwan Semiconductor Manufacturing Corporation TSMC to build factories in the US. In 2023, it was years ahead of other manufacturers when it came to producing the smallest and fastest microchips. We see a dual strategy by the US government here: promoting its own skills and attracting foreign skills[109].

Strategies with Rear-View Mirror Perspective

During the seminar, the participants develop three strategies for their respective scenario, which indicate the specific result to have been achieved in the target year of the scenario. This also includes three tactics for each of the strategies that show how the strategies can be realistically implemented.

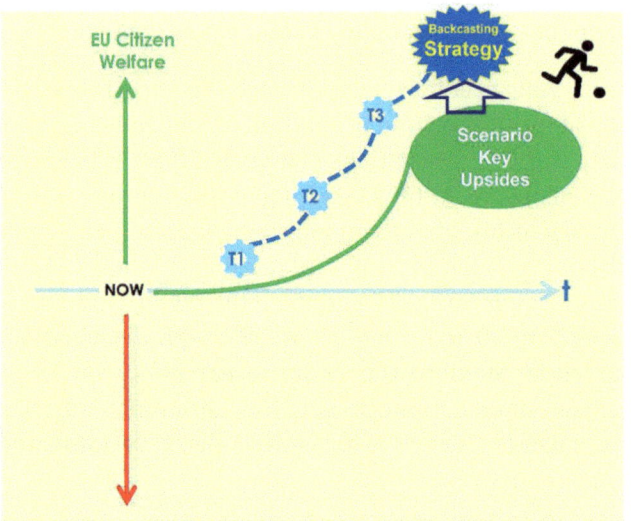

The tactics show the path from the current to the desired realization date as challenging but achievable. For example, a gradual phase-out of cars with combustion engines could reduce the proportion of registrations from 100% to over 70% and from 30% to 0% over several years.

But watch out, Europe. What looks good now may turn out to be disastrous for the EU. Why? The Norwegian economy does not feature a domestic manufacturer of cars with combustion engines. On the other hand, the economies of several

European countries depend on the continued wellbeing of car manufacturers. Merely prohibiting cars with combustion engines without simultaneously invigorating and protecting the domestic car manufacturers during a transitional period may turn into economic disaster for the European economy as we indicated earlier. Incentives and disincentives are powerful tools that can have disastrous and unwanted consequences if used without a view to the complex interdependencies in whole systems. Henry Louis Mencken was right: *"For every complex problem there is a solution that is clear, simple and wrong."* EU regulators beware!

Implementing strategies in several steps helps the client to recognize that the recommended strategy is feasible for her and can be implemented. In politics, it can help voters to understand and accept the desired changes. Even painful decisions are accepted by voters – if they are implemented with a delay of two legislative periods, i.e., have no negative effects on the voters yet during the next election.

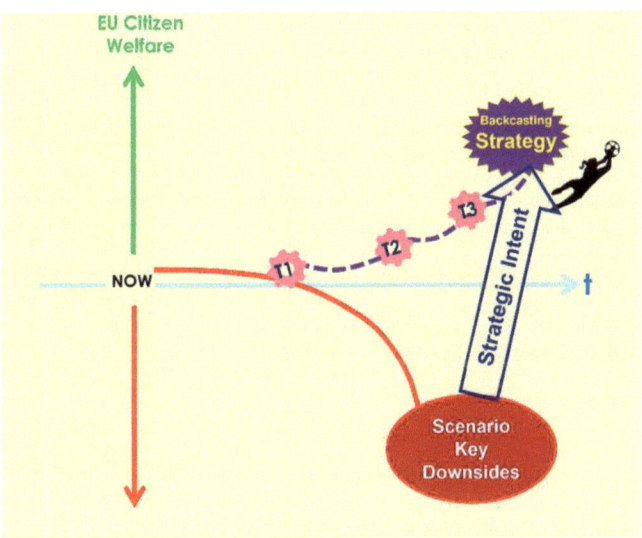

If the strategic goal is clear, but not the tactical steps for how to achieve it, then two different paths are available: Design thinking and positive deviation.

Design thinking goes back to the way Steve Jobs worked and initially produced a prototype of the desired solution, tried it out and improved it repeatedly until the right solution was realized. Steve Jobs is said to have carried a prototype of the iPhone in his trouser pocket, together with his car keys, which scratched the prototype's screen. This is how he realized that the iPhone needed a glass screen that would neither scratch nor break under normal use. We will meet Design Thinking again in chapter 3.1 on the topic of personal career planning.

The Positive Deviance approach is based on the conviction that there are always innovative solutions, even for complex problems. We just have not identified them yet and have not helped them achieve a breakthrough[110] . There often are people who already practice these solutions with success but are ignored by mainstream society for a variety of reasons, in part because their solutions may go against current cultural standards. They prefer not to expose themselves to ridicule or other social marginalization. Positive Deviance as a method was developed by Richard Pasquale, Jerry and Monique Sternin[111] and has proven to be helpful in solving even seemingly intractable problems in societies around the world.

The most impressive example was the overcoming of hunger-related child mortality in Vietnam in the early 1990s through the unconventional use of available local resources. Jerry and Monique Sternin initially searched for poor parents in the particularly affected regions whose children remained healthy. They met with them and accompanied them in their daily routines. During that process, they discovered behaviors and perspectives that led to a significant reduction in hunger in Vietnam, albeit with some tactics beyond local cultural norms at the time. The Sternins built trust with and included all local authorities, village elders and parents in the region to jointly legitimize these discovered solutions and thus transform them into new acceptable cultural norms and habits for the benefit of the health of all children[112] .

Both options are only addressed as possibilities in the seminar.

Three Scenario-Specific Strategies

In the Scenario Planning Extreme seminar and project, strategies for the scenarios are developed in the following steps:

- Identification of one of the main threats or opportunities for the client
- Definition of the desired strategic result
- Identification of three tactics that lead to the desired result.

Just as in the case of scenario imaginating, each scenario team member partners with someone from another scenario and presents the results. As described above for the development of scenarios, the partners give encouraging feedback to each other and suggest concrete and specific improvement opportunities recognized by them. After the mutual consultation, the participants return to their scenario teams and improve their first takes on strategy and tactics. This mutual consultation approach to scenario and strategy development has proven to be particularly useful in our seminars.

The teams then each develop two further strategies with tactics that deal with the opportunities and risks of their respective scenarios.

Step 8:
Scenario Alert Signals

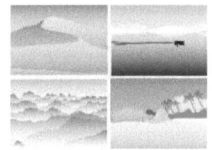

Have the courage to
use and trust your own mind.
Immanuel Kant

*S*cenario Planning Extreme deliberately explores extreme possible futures. Its purpose is not to predict these futures but to prepare the client by alerting them to signals that indicate when the appropriate strategies for success should be initiated.

How can I, as a client, recognize when the time has come for a particular scenario and that implementing the strategies I have prepared for this eventuality is the right course of action? The answer lies in signals—subtle indicators that serve as early harbingers of the scenario. These signals, however, are often overlooked or recognized too late. The reason for this delay lies in the characteristics of our influencing Siamese Twins: our inseparable reality tunnel and meaning of life. These cognitive filters make it easy to interpret even threatening signals in our environment in ways that align with our pre-existing perceptions, thereby reinforcing and confirming our reality tunnels rather than challenging them.

A fitting metaphor for this phenomenon is the frog in the cooking pot: as the water is slowly heated, the frog remains sitting in the pot, despite the slowly rising temperature. Failing to recognize the danger, it does not jump out to save itself. Do we believe that people would never act as irrationally as the frog? Experience shows that, all too often, they would.

In 1980, a historic volcanic explosion occurred on Mount St. Helens in the State of Oregon, releasing over a cubic kilometer of ash and debris into the sky. The entire northern flank of the mountain collapsed, burying everything in its path. Two months before the eruption, the north side of the mountain began to expand, signaling an impending disaster. When the threat became critical, the authorities ordered the local population to leave their homes and evacuate immediately. Everyone complied—except for Harry R. Truman, the 83-year-old owner of Spirit Lake Lodge, a tourist accommodation located near the mountain. Tragically, both Truman and his small hotel lodge were buried by the eruption of the mountain under the volcanic debris. Posthumously, Truman became famous as a symbol of defiance and loyalty to his home. [113] There is something deeply sympathetic about Harry R. Truman's story, which may explain why he even has a German-language Wikipedia entry covering his story.[114]

Our Siamese Twins become our enemies when they conflict with reality. This is the essence of extreme 1926ing, leading us all the way straight into disaster. If we become emotionally attached enough to our current version of our reality tunnels, we risk suffering economic consequences, or even worse outcomes.

To avoid such fates, we need a metaphorical thermometer, something that alerts us when it is time to change course decisively. However, it is critical to identify these alert signals before the moment of action arrives. In a playful "what if" learning situation, this becomes emotionally easier for us because it feels like a game, not a threat. In such a context, our Siamese Twins do not feel challenged or endangered.

What characterizes a good scenario alert signal? It should be present and recognizable in everyday life for those who remain observant and open-minded. In a variation of the principle of Positive Deviation, we can say that these unobtrusive indicators for scenario alert signals are always already present. They just need to be noted.

How do we recognize them? Scenario alert signals are identified by detecting out-of-the-ordinary changes in key trends within a scenario. For example, in Shell's scenario planning about the future of OPEC, the company identified unusual reductions in the price of crude oil traded on the London Stock Exchange as a critical signal. As part of the scenario planning project, Shell determined that if the price of crude oil fell below a specified trigger level, it would only be a matter of time before the OPEC cartel ceased to function as a mechanism for reduced oil production. This would lead to global oil production aligning more closely to keep pace with market demand from consuming countries.

A valuable scenario alert signal possesses the following properties:
- Public Accessibility: The information is readily available to the public.
- Credible Sources: It is reported by reputable media outlets, such as CBS, Wall Street Journal, Washington Post.
- Scenario Relevance: It directly pertains to a specific core threat or core opportunity within the scenario.
- Exponential Deviation: It indicates a significant, accelerating departure from the expected trend.

During the seminar, scenario teams develop three distinct scenario alert signals for each scenario. For example, a scenario alert signal for a study on a radical new future of personal mobility previously discussed above, could be the 2023 authorization of autonomous taxi cabs in more than a dozen major U.S. cities.

While identifying scenario alert signals may seem challenging from today's perspective, it becomes much easier to recognize them when viewed retrospectively from within the perspective of the possible extreme scenario itself. Most teams find it straightforward to recognize and name effective scenario wake-up signals when they adopt the perspective of being "inside" the future scenario.

Identifying Supporters for Our Strategies
The most important supporters in implementing strategies are pioneering trend-setters. Organizations need individuals who identify as trendsetters to champion

their strategies and drive their success. Steve Jobs excelled at cultivating a fan base that enthusiastically embraced new products, bringing Apple worldwide attention, global recognition, and ensuring rapid acceptance and adoption of its innovations. His iconic style of product launches—complete with dramatic presentations in packed congress halls, carefully curated formats, an invited audience, and his signature informal attire—has become a template for many entrepreneurs. Today, you can see echoes of his approach in the presentations of decision-makers at Google, Apple, AMD, NVIDIA, or Elon Musk. The hallmark of a great idea is still imitation by others, including CEOs.

Social changes of all kinds, including the adoption of revolutionary products and services, rarely take place suddenly, but rather gradually over time. The normal distribution of change over time can be visualized as a caravan moving through the desert. Our illustration depicts this process, dividing the population into four separate groups, which together collectively form the well-known bell curve.

Time Caravan of Social Change

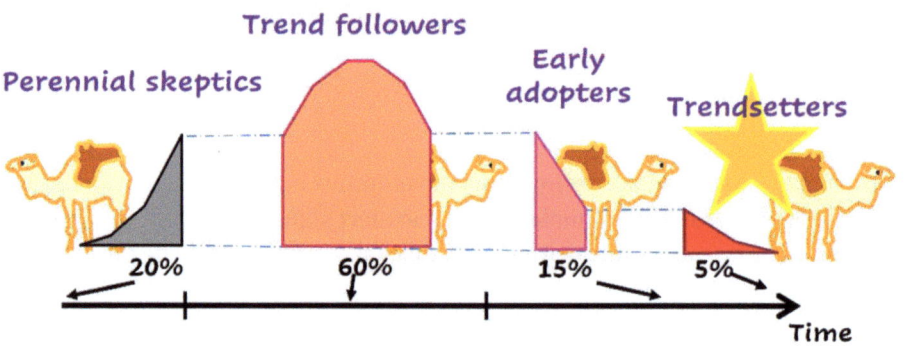

At the forefront of the caravan of social change are approximately five percent of the relevant community who identify as true **Trendsetters,** individuals eager to co-create and lead change[115].

Following them are the **Early adopters** who join follow with some delay but are open to innovation. The vast majority comes next, who we label **Trend followers**, adopting the change after some additional time and persuasion. Finally, at the end of the caravan of change are the **Perennial skeptics**, those who resist change, preferring to maintain the status quo. This group follows reluctantly, only after significant delays and external pressure. When it comes to successfully and swiftly introducing innovative products or services, and to influencing public opinion, the trendsetters are the most important group to engage and inspire.

During a scenario project, it is worthwhile identifying potential trendsetters who may already exist and consider how they can be approached, engaged, and won over as a future fan base for communicating and implementing the strategies. Their support could significantly accelerate the desired changes, both in terms of time and content.

This approach is equally relevant in the fields of politics and public administration. When implementing strategies and tactics that may encounter resistance later, it can be important to look out for and secure future advocates early on. These supporters can play a pivotal role in shaping public opinion to align with the objectives of the scenario strategy. For politicians, whose success often hinges on public sentiment, having such forward-thinking allies can not only enhance their ability to sway public opinion but also embolden them to make more decisive and courageous choices. This future-orientated planning can often be the determining factor between winning and losing an election.

Step 9:
Winning Over the Client

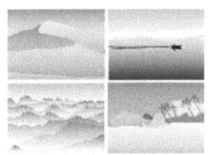

Help me
to do it myself.
Maria Montessori

*M*aria Montessori is often described as the "master builder of education," even for the poorest of the poor. She developed the principles of learning that emphasize self-learning—self-directed education. Martin's son Daniel attended a Montessori kindergarten for two years, starting at the age of three, and quickly internalized this principle. Whenever Daniel needed help and Martin wanted to show him how to do something, Daniel would firmly interrupt him with the words: *"Let! Me!"*

How can I convince my client? We can approach this using Maria Montessori's concept of self-determination: How do I help my client to recognize what is in her best interest and empower her to decide for herself?

The External Seminar

The external seminar Scenario Planning Extreme is designed as a simulation in which participants simulate the role of consultants to the EU Commission. Their task is to develop scenarios and appropriate corresponding strategies for succeeding within those scenarios. At the conclusion of the seminar, participants meet with simulated client representatives to present their analysis and recommendations. The goal is to actively involve the client representatives in the process, thus transforming them into co-consultants for the client.

This "winning over the client" takes place in the seminar room, surrounded by the participants' workshop materials, including all the flipcharts, storyboards, and film posters the team produced. Following a few brief introductory words from the seminar facilitator outlining the format of the seminar and the steps of the Scenario Planning Extreme journey, each of the four scenario teams delivers their presentation. Every team member has approximately three minutes to present their part of the analysis and recommendations.

The German American pioneer of organizational development, Kurt Lewin[116], identified the optimal way to win people over to a new solution. This process involves three key steps:

1. **Unfreezing**: Traditional habits, often deeply cherished, are "unfrozen" by challenging the status quo and creating awareness of the need for change.
2. **Changing:** New behaviors are introduced, recognized, discussed, and accepted through collaborative group work. In this phase, the old behaviors are exchanged by new ones.
3. **Refreezing:** The group agrees to implement the new behaviors in practice, solidifying and embedding them as the new norm.

In Scenario Planning Extreme, the **unfreezing** phase is achieved through the client's initial openness to conduct such a project and by introducing scenarios that

136

starkly contrast with the client's current situation. These scenarios highlight indications that the client's existing success recipes are likely to fail under future conditions. The **change** involves the client identifying and considering the recommended strategies along with the scenario alert signals that will guide their response to the potential future challenges or opportunities. The **refreezing** phase occurs when the client accepts and later implements the strategies tied to the specific scenarios, triggered by the respective alert signals.

We will now explore how these three steps are applied in external seminars and subsequently in in-house projects.

Unfreeze: At the beginning of their presentation, the team members articulate in their own words how their understanding of the EU's overarching accountability is for supporting its citizens. They explain the key strategic question as they developed during the seminar, focusing on the EU's roles. Starting the meeting in this way demonstrates to the client that the consultants not only understand but also support their accountabilities, beginning to open the client to the seminar's purpose.

The scenario teams then describe the extreme changes that the EU could eventually face in relation to the strategic question. These major changes and new challenges serve to "unfreeze" the client's current solutions and encourage openness to the possibilities of change.

Client representatives are presented with insights into the relevant trend groups and recognize the potential exponential shifts these trends could bring over the next 25 years. Each team describes the seven key trends within their scenario, including which black swans have triggered what sudden changes. The presentations are delivered from the perspective of the future, where the scenario team members guide the clients to "look back" at the present from their specific scenarios. This approach vividly illustrates the need for innovative solutions and underscores the importance of adapting to potential future challenges.

Change: The scenario teams demonstrate the positive effects of the new strategies they have developed for their respective scenarios. They highlight the advantages of their recommendations and present their scenario alert signals, which serve as are harbingers of the potential of their respective scenarios unfolding.

Following the presentations, the clients are invited to provide feedback and suggestions to refine the scenarios and strategies, ensuring they are more aligned with the client's expectations and approval. Their comments and recommendations are written on post-its notes and attached to the storyboards or the corresponding strategy flipcharts. These inputs are then incorporated into the written final reports of the various scenario teams as considerations for a future version 2.0. This collaborative process transforms the clients into active participants within the scenario teams, fostering a sense of shared ownership and engagement in the outcomes.

Re-freeze: Client representatives are invited to become part of the team responsible for winning over the decision makers. The scenario teams also offer suggestions for implementing the strategies within the client's organization. These suggestions include:

- Assigning a responsibility for monitoring trends that could impact strategic issues,
- Repeating the study at regular intervals, such as annually,
- Tracking the various scenario alert signals to enable timely implementation of scenario-specific strategies, and
- Identifying and building trust with potential future supporters to facilitate the adoption of scenario strategies.

Informal personal meetings between consultants and client representatives following the formal presentations play a crucial role. These conversations often have the strongest impact on shaping the personal attitudes of both seminar participants and clients, fostering trust and deeper engagement.

The final day of the seminar is dedicated to authoring the final reports in collaboration with all seminar participants. Each scenario team drafts a detailed report on its scenario, with individual team members contributing the sections they presented orally. These individual contributions are integrated into a coherent document, which also includes photos of their posters and storyboards, which were created during the seminar. This marks the conclusion of their work.

Winning Over the Internal Client

The Montessori principle *"Help me to do it myself"* also applies when convincing the internal client: *How do I help her to recognize, on her own, what is in her best interest and decide to act on it?*

138

Communicating the value of Scenario Planning Extreme and its results to the client is quite different from selling a product. It is about addressing the client's self-image, her future, and her ability to thrive in a time of ever accelerating and profound change.

When it comes to issues affecting the viability of the client's organization, her Siamese Twins—their reality tunnel perspective inseparably linked to their meaning of existence —are on high alert. In an increasingly uncertain world, she expects the identified strategies to assure her organization's sustainability and relevance, in even extreme futures. These strategies must demonstrate that they protect and strengthen:

- Her loyalties,
- The things she holds dear,
- The people she cares about,
- Her values,
- the meaning of her existence, and
- Her relevant communities.

She wants to see and needs assurance that, even in extreme futures, her organization will not merely survive but also continue to make positive contributions to society. These contributions, while potentially different from those of the present, remain consistent with her self-image, financially viable and attractive, and supportive of long-term future growth.

In other words, the challenge is this: *How do we win over the client and her organization to embrace this approach?*

Co-Creating Scenarios

The process of winning over the client begins right at the start of the project. The client—typically the CEO and her decision makers, participates in describing the organization's self-image, purpose, and values. They are also involved in formulating the strategic question for the planned Scenario Planning Extreme study. Additionally, they should be asked about the trends they perceive in their environment that are relevant to the strategic question, both encouraging and concerning.

At the conclusion of the Scenario Planning Extreme project, the scenarios and the methodology are presented to the client. This presentation is most effective when it features the actual posters, flipcharts and storyboards produced during the project. We strongly advise against elegant electronic polished presentations, which risk fading quickly by being forgotten amidst the endless chain of PowerPoint presentation slides already circulating within the organization.

Years of experience in organizational development reveal that physical materials, such as paper, carry a unique convincing power. They demonstrate authenticity by showing that the work has been created by real people whom the client knows personally. Hand-drawn movie posters in flipchart size spark our curiosity, conveying that this is not a generic, cut-and-paste product, but the result of genuine convictions from respected colleagues. Scenarios depicted on oversized storyboards—four times the size of flipcharts—and presented with conviction by their creators feel alive and compelling. Storyboards grab clients' attention by engaging it in ways digital presentations cannot.

Another advantage of using paper is that it signals that the results are deliberately still prototypes, thereby intentionally leaving plenty of room for the client's questions and suggestions. This format invites the client to become a co-creator and co-owner of both the process and the results, fostering a sense of shared commitment and ownership of the approach.

Since 2022, AI-generated computer images shaped by creative prompts seem to be winning the attention of image-hungry audiences. Have you participated yet in a prompt battle to create the most attractive image for a given topic? The winning images can look quite cool. So why not use them for creating compelling scenario movie posters as well? This raises the important question: *What is the purpose of the movie poster in Scenario Planning Extreme?*

There are two key reasons:

1. Creating a vision of extreme but possible futures: The first purpose is to present an image of extreme yet potential future scenarios that do not overwhelm the client. Hand-drawn movie posters do not really scare anyone—they have the unique advantage of being engaging while not intimidating. In contrast, AI-generated computer images can sometimes overwhelm the viewers. The goal is to take the client on a personal journey she will enjoy, one that sparks curiosity rather than fear. In this sense, hand drawings score 1:0 over AI images.

2. Demonstrating team ownership, commitment, and authenticity: The second purpose is to show that the scenarios were created by a real team of committed partners. Hand drawn posters reflect the team members' personal investment and motivation. Posters illustrate that the participants are not just designers of the scenarios but also committed partners ready to help implement the strategies successfully. While slick prompt-generated AI images are visually impressive, they are impersonal and do not connect the client nor the project participants to the scenarios in a personal way. Clients and participants are unlikely to recognize themselves as real contributors to such images. The overall result: Hand drawings score 2:0 over AI images. They more effectively resonate with our reality tunnels, connecting us to real people, their ideas, and their commitments. This principle aligns with Amazon founder Jeff Bezos' rules for effective meetings, which famously exclude PowerPoint presentations[117]. The emphasis is on real, human-centered engagement, rather than polished but impersonal visuals.

Unlike typical seminars, where it is customary to tear up and throw away flipcharts and other materials at the end of the event, Scenario Planning Extreme values preserving these materials. They can be reused in later follow-up meetings with decision makers, providing continuity and reinforcing the strategies. In international organizations, this approach can even take on a "relay race" style, where successive seminars across different geographic location build upon each other. In such cases, flipcharts and other materials are carried across countries and continents to achieve strategic rethinking at top management level. Martin personally witnessed that at AMD, where this approach led to remarkable results.

Ideally, the first presentation to the client focuses on primarily helping them understand how the scenarios were developed. This includes explaining the trends characterizing the scenarios, and which black swans accelerated change. The client thereby discovers and gains insight into how various potential future worlds came about and recognizes their origins and roots in present-day trends.

After the scenario presentation, the client will naturally wish to begin right away discussing strategic solutions for these scenarios. While it may be tempting for the team members to address solutions immediately, we strongly advise against it. It is crucial to first clarify any questions about the methodology, convey the logic behind the scenarios, and ensure that all client questions are thoroughly addressed. If decision-makers feel their concerns are not fully answered, there is a significant risk that the project could lose momentum or stall entirely thereby coming to a halt.

Another potential challenge is if the client wants to exclude the most negative scenario, dismissing it from further consideration as too unlikely. This reaction must be avoided at all costs. It is often a symptom of suppressing issues that are perceived as extremely threatening to their Siamese Twins. In such cases, it helps to point out that the negative scenario is just one of four potential futures and that identifying strategies to successfully deal with it is a critical part of the process. The client should also be invited to think about how their current strategies would fare in future contexts. Would the current "recipes for success" remain effective in extreme scenarios? This reflection helps to underscore the need for adaptive and transformative strategies to navigate even the most challenging scenarios.

This takes time. Martin recalls his early days at AMD when he proposed a new type of personnel program. Eager and highly motivated, he signaled to his boss, Stan,[118] that he was ready to present the idea to the executive committee for approval. Why wait? However, Stan, an extraordinary diplomat, asked for patience. He understood how to navigate the organization to get things done better than Martin, who came from a management consultancy background. For six weeks, Stan and Martin repeatedly met and worked together on the proposal, reviewing, and refining the presentation, often suggesting what seemed to Martin like unimportant rewordings. This went on for six weeks. Then Martin was able to present the concept. It was approved right away. What happened during those six weeks? Stan personally met with each of his fellow board members, discussed the proposal with them, and gratefully accepted even the smallest suggestions for improvement. After each meeting he explained to Martin why it was worth incorporating each board member's input, one by one, no matter how minor. By the time Martin finally presented the proposal to the executive committee, each member recognized their own suggested changes, however small, reflected in the concept. This created a sense of shared ownership, ensuring support, and the proposal was approved immediately. Stan had effectively made the proposal theirs now, not just Martin's. He knew and practiced an essential rule of organizational dynamics: committee decisions are made before the formal decision-making meetings. By engaging the key decision-makers in the process and making them all co-owners of the proposal, Stan demonstrated what we call successive prototyping—a method of gradually building buy-in with the key people whose support is critical to reach approval for implementation. This example highlights truly superb diplomacy at work! It demonstrates why it is well worth working closely with key co-deciders of strategic change in organizations.

When the client tests her current solutions in the various future scenarios and realizes that they have a low chance of success, she becomes more open to the project team's suggested strategies. The same applies to the scenario alert signals and ideas for identifying early supporters described in step eight. In fact, the client may eventually contribute some of the best suggestions on these issues.

The project is successful when the client recognizes that the recommended strategies are both challenging and achievable. Success is further augmented when the client sees that the strategies fit the organization, living up to its values, strengthening its position, and preparing it for the future—even if this means replacing some of its currently successful products and services with new ones.

This marks the conclusion of the first phase of a scenario project, which is often externally facilitated. Success at this stage means that the client has not only recognized the value of Scenario Planning Extreme but has also accepted the recommendations. She will now use them within the organization and take appropriate steps to prepare for the possible implementation of strategies once the scenario alert signals indicate the time is right. When the time to act arrives, the client will be ready with well-prepared strategies, enabling her organization to act decisively thereby translating into competitive advantage.[119]

Step 10:
Implementing Scenario Planning Extreme

Do or do not.
There is no try.
Yoda in the movie "Star Wars
The Empire Strikes Back."

In the previous chapter, we explored how to carefully win over the client to Scenario Planning Extreme, step by step. Let us now assume that we have been successful, and the client looks at us and asks: What needs to happen next?

Just as every individual is unique, so is every HuLiO (Human Like Organization). Each organization must find its own course to implement the recommendations, finding a path that aligns with its unique structure, culture, and values.

Implementing strategies may sound straightforward in theory, but in practice, it can be challenging. Scenario Planning Extreme requires a balance of head, heart, and hand:

- o **Head,** because intelligent and strategic thinking is essential for effective implementation.
- o **Heart**, because extreme scenarios and strategies intentionally explore worlds far removed from the status quo, demanding emotional resilience and openness.
- o **Hand**, because implementation ventures into uncharted territory, where prior experience offers limited guidance.

In Part One of this book, we described the failures of IBM with the PC, AT&T with the cell phone, and Nokia with the iPhone. In Chapter 1.3, we posed the question: Could these three companies have avoided their mistakes if they had consulted Scenario Planning Extreme on these issues. From this perspective, the answer is a resounding "Yes, And". What does the "And" signify? It underscores that using Scenario Planning Extreme's recommendations involves far more than simply approving budgets and delegating implementation tasks to various departments and groups. The "And" represents the deeper commitment and transformative effort required for success.

The implementation process within organizations can be divided into two groups of interconnected tasks:

1. Preparing for extreme scenarios and their strategies: This involves initiative-taking measures to ensure readiness for the identified scenarios, as well as the ability to execute the strategies effectively when needed.
2. Expand the organization's self-image and reality tunnel: Organizations must open themselves up to thinking in terms of extreme scenarios, innovative future strategies, and success principles of the learning organization. At the same time, they must clarify and affirm their core values, ensuring these remain central even as they adapt to new realities.

Scenario Planning Extreme thus challenges organizations to embrace new ways of thinking and acting, enabling them not only to survive but to thrive in complex and rapidly changing environments.

Preparing for extreme scenarios involves several critical tasks that ensure the organization is ready to respond effectively when one of these scenarios begins to unfold. The tasks include the following:

1. Detailed elaboration of strategies: Each proposed strategy for the scenarios must be thoroughly developed, addressing key questions such as:
   o What resources are required for implementation?
   o How will the strategies be financed?
   o How should personnel be organized to support these efforts?

This process requires extensive coordination and alignment involving both the line and staff functions within the organization. The time invested in these discussions ensures that the strategies will be practical and actionable.

2. Continuous monitoring of the scenario alert signals: Organizations must establish systems to monitor alert signals thereby triggering the implementation of the corresponding prepared strategies when one of the scenarios begins to materialize. However, in the daily stress and pressure of urgent tasks, these alert signals are easily overlooked. For example, in Shell's scenario, the decline of the oil price on the London Stock Exchange below a pre-determined level was the trigger for the "end of the oil embargo" scenario, a signal that appeared as a small note in a financial daily newspaper. Most managers had "better things to do" than keeping an eye on them. This should fall to a monitoring group that ensures these signals are not missed.

3. Annual update of the Scenario Planning Extreme study: Repeating and updating the study annually is essential. This process involves revising scenarios, refining strategies, and discussing them with the relevant managers in the organization. By engaging managers as co-creators, the organization strengthens ownership of the scenarios and their corresponding strategies. Fostering alignment and commitment.

4. Expanding the organization's self-image and updating the Reality Tunnel: We saw in Chapter 1.3 that extreme scenarios deliberately trigger a *contrast effect* with clients, shaking up traditional thinking and opening many possibilities for the future. This is crucial for preventing the organization's current reality tunnels from continuing to act as blinkers, blinding it from perceiving the risks and challenges in the present, while limiting its ability to take their available opportunities seriously. Extreme scenarios allow the organization's Siamese Twins to playfully fail and recognize

that the solutions lie in adopting the proposed strategies resulting from the expanded self-image and reality tunnels. Insights gained through Scenario Planning Extreme, and the learning of the Siamese Twins go hand in hand—or not at all.

5. Distinguishing values from products/services: Successful and sustainable "living" organizations, as described by Arie de Geus, make a clear distinction between their long-term values and purpose and the products and services they currently offer. In a constantly evolving world, the needs, wants, opportunities, and challenges of organizations and their various stakeholders also change, necessitating fresh solutions. An organization that seeks to become and remain sustainable must take this into account and continually innovate and improve its offerings to meet the changing demands of its clients and the public. At the same time, the organization's core values must be preserved and strengthened, remaining intact because they serve as the guiding compass for organizational decision-making and action. When the organization's values are seen as inseparable from, or too closely tied to its products and services, they risk becoming barriers to growth and adaptability.

Consider IBM's historical challenge with the personal computer (PC), which it invented, and the question of its future. The corporation, which saw itself primarily as a manufacturer of mainframe computers, initially conceived the PC as an input device for those systems. However, extreme scenario planning could have revealed the PC's potential as a revolutionary product for individual consumers, opening an entire, giant new market for IBM. Had IBM expanded its self-image to include the consumer market—while still maintaining its stronghold in the computer mainframe market—it might have better recognized the extraordinary potential of its PC. This highlights the importance of maintaining organizational values while remaining flexible in adapting to new markets and opportunities.

The same principle applies to Intel's initiative with massive parallel computing using massively parallel PC cores as an alternative to mainframes. Had IBM expanded its self-image from being solely a provider of mainframes to position itself as a provider of XXL computing capacities, it might have been able to capitalize on this wave of innovation more effectively and more quickly than Intel.

What happened at AT&T with cell phones? Instead of relying on quantitative market potential estimates based on trend extrapolations by external consultants, a Scenario Planning Extreme project could have enabled AT&T to *imaginate* a future world where cell phones were universally available and affordable—not just in the US, but globally. This broader conceptual expansion might have led AT&T to reposition itself as the dominant player in not just domestic, but also global communication markets. A common mistake many companies make is measuring the potential of innovative ideas by comparing the sales volumes of new products and services with those of mature ones, using an arithmetic instead of a geometric perspective. This approach often results in a significant underestimation of an innovation's potential. Even many in-house generated innovative ideas in large corporations do not stand a chance for precisely this reason. Take the invention of PCs with graphical interface tools: the latter were invented not by Apple but by Xerox, which defined itself narrowly as a "document company", thereby missing the broader market potential of its innovation.

Nokia is our third example of missed opportunities. Let us imagine for a moment if Nokia had conducted an extreme scenario study on the potential of the iPhone and recognized the enormous long-term market potential it represented. Such a study would likely have led to the development of various strategies. One of these would probably have been to expand Nokia's Symbian operating system to match the capabilities of the iPhone—an attempt that ultimately failed miserably. Another viable strategy could have been to acquire the Android operating system, which was up for sale at the time. Nokia could have pursued both paths simultaneously, allowing them to compete for success over a pre-defined period. This dual-path approach has been a successful strategy employed by organizations including the SONY Group and Microsoft for decades. In Nokia's case, the organization could have leveraged both systems: opting to use the Android operating system for smartphones while continuing to use the Symbian system for traditional cell phones. This dual strategy could have enabled Nokia to maintain its existing market dominance while positioning itself for long-term growth in the emerging smartphone market.

Commitment to "both/and." Adopting a "both/and" perspective can significantly ease the emotional expansion of both the individual's self-image and the organization's reality tunnel. This mindset embraces dualities, recognizing that seemingly opposing needs can exist. For example, consumers often want both a landline and a mobile phone connection, reflecting how different solutions can complement one another.

Form follows function. The organization's structure should align with its tasks and objectives. In many companies, responsibility for short and medium-term planning often lies with the finance department, which makes sense given the highly quantitative nature of this type of planning. However, Scenario Planning Extreme, which is based primarily on qualitative data and imaginating, can be an anathema for the quantitative experts of the organization, clashing with their quantitative mindset and methods. Such differences in methodology often lead to conflicts. To avoid these clashes, it makes sense to establish a separate dedicated Scenario Planning Extreme group. It should ideally report directly to a major line function within the organization. Arie de Geus, for instance, described how accountability for the Shell scenario planning group rotated between different line functions, with the executive in charge of this function providing leadership. Consistent with this logic, all employment at the extraordinarily successful DARPA operates on a rotational basis, limiting all appointments to five years. Using the principal of rotational employment ensures fresh perspectives and adaptability, aligning well with the dynamic needs of scenario planning and fostering a culture of both innovation and accountability.

The organization's efforts to expand its self-image and improve its reality tunnel are best assigned to the Organizational Development group, as these initiatives align directly with its core accountabilities.

Building a network of internal scenario extreme trendsetters drawn from all areas of the organization fosters cross-functional collaboration, strengthens their mutual commitment and sparks creativity to generate ideas on how to address newly discovered challenges. The inclusion of diverse perspectives enriches potential solutions, while the network itself becomes a mental space of protective solidarity— a safeguard in times when internal perennial skeptics attempt to stop or marginalize the change process.

The leaders responsible for Scenario Planning Extreme should actively promote networking between internal and external trendsetters. Leveraging the experience and insights of external innovators can often lead to faster and more cost-effective progress than relying solely on internal experimentation. Why limit the search for innovative ideas to within the organization? Often the seeds of groundbreaking ideas originate externally.

External trendsetters, far from being competitors who envy each other, thrive on sharing their methodological insights and engaging with others in meaningful discussions. This openness not only strengthens their own thinking but contributes to the overall evolution of ideas and methods. By fostering external networking, the organization can tap into a broader pool of innovation, enriching its own processes while accelerating growth and adaptability.

A wonderful example of organizational developers' willingness to collaborate across organizational boundaries is the compendium of ideas compiled by Mary Lynn Manns and Linda Rising in their book *Fearless Change: Patterns for the Introduction of New Ideas*[120] . This highlights strategies that have proven successful in driving organizational change and fostering innovation across diverse settings.

Black Swan Events and Scenario Planning Extreme—Black Swan events have the power to compress decades years into a single year. Scenario Planning Extreme, which develops scenarios set 25 years into the future, offers a vital framework for breaking free from the constraints of the status quo. By extending the outlook so far into the future, it becomes easier to imagine radical departures from current realities- After all, hardly anyone would that the world will not undergo dramatic transformations in the next 25 years. This long-term 25-year perspective acts as our license to think about and explore extreme scenarios with greater freedom.

However, we must also remain aware that the future often arrives far more rapidly than anticipated. What seems distant and far in the future can become reality the day after tomorrow. A striking example of how quickly technology can reshape industries and societies is artificial intelligence. Just think of the radical shift triggered by ChatGPT in November 2022.

Acting Now: Small Bets and Preventative Action—Sometimes, it pays to place small, strategic side bets right now. This is particularly true for threat scenarios, where taking some early preventative action aligns with the principle of the motto: prevention is better than cure. Taking initial steps today can mitigate risks and set the stage for effective responses should the scenario materialize later.

In Chapter 3.2 on migration and integration, we will explore how some of these strategies can be implemented immediately and why initiative-taking measures in this area are especially valuable. Preparing now for potential challenges strengthens organizations' resilience and positions us to adapt effectively to future realities.

How do you become a Living Organization? In his book, Arie De Geus paints an attractive picture of the Living Organization—one that operates with resilience, adaptability, and long-term perspective. Who would not want their organization to follow these principles? The answer, of course, is that we all do. So why is this approach not universally practiced?

The answer lies in the question of the ownership structures of the organizations. Most living organizations are either family-owned or structured as foundations, which allows them to think in terms of generations rather than focusing on quarterly results. In contrast, publicly traded companies, particularly those that are listed on the New York Stock Exchange, face a far different reality. Here, the average shareholding lasts just six months,[121] and shareholders are often driven by the desire for continuous share price increases. This creates considerable pressure on management to deliver short-term financial success, often at the expense of long-term sustainability.

The Role of Reputable Investment Funds—Some reputable investment funds mitigate this pressure by supporting companies that consciously and reliably pursue long-term strategies. These funds help protect businesses from shareholders solely interested in short-term gains. Nevertheless, the temptation for listed companies to prioritize the demands of short-term investors remains significant. This issue is particularly pronounced in companies that recruit their CEOs from external sources. Leaders appointed from outside the company may feel pressured to maximize short-term profits, even if that severely undermines the organization's long-term capabilities. In some cases, such CEOs have left behind weakened organizations while moving on to new executive roles elsewhere.

De Geus' Advice: *Prioritize Internal Leadership*—De Geus advocates for companies to prioritize internal candidates for CEO positions wherever possible. Leaders who have grown within the organization are more likely to align with their long-term vision and values. They understand the organization's core mission and are less likely to sacrifice sustainable growth for short-term gains.

Success Together in Every Future— Scenario Planning Extreme equips users to prepare for all possible futures. It enables committed individuals to imagine dramatic trends, understand their potential effects on the organization, and collaboratively develop answers. This approach works best when it brings together people with divergent perspectives and convictions, fostering an environment where they see themselves as equal partners in finding solutions rooted in shared values. Most importantly, ideas only become reality when they are understood and embraced by the decision-makers. Their involvement as co-creators and thus co-owners of the final strategies ensures both acceptance and commitment to their successful implementation.

Every Path is a New Path—The poet and illustrator Wilhelm Busch once said: " Those who walk in the footsteps of others leave no trace of their own." The suggestions in this chapter should be understood in this sense. Each organization is unique and must discover its own path to its specific goals. While the strategies shared here provide inspiration, it is up to every organization to adapt and innovate in ways that align with its own identity and objectives.

The Infinite Journey of Evolution—The evolution of humanity is an endless journey, shaped primarily by our own actions. How long each of us partakes in it depends on the choices we make. The same holds true for organizations and societies. Their longevity is determined by their ability to learn and adapt together. Collaboration, creativity, and commitment to growth are the keys to longevity and thriving in an ever-changing world.

By adopting these principles, organizations can move closer to becoming Living Organizations, balancing profitability with resilience, adaptability, and a long-term perspective that benefits all stakeholders.

Part III:
Coping with an Extreme World

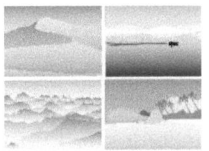

Gray, dear friend,
is all theory.
Mephisto in "Faust"
Johann Wolfgang v. Goethe

*S*cenario Planning Extreme opens our eyes and broadens our perspective by preparing us for extreme eventualities on a global scale. Part III presents three illustrative examples of this.

Can I use Scenario Planning Extreme for my own career aspirations? Yes. Absolutely. Just as organizations can benefit from using Scenario Planning Extreme to prepare for extreme futures, individuals can apply the same principles to their

personal life planning. Chapter 3.1 offers some suggestions for this. After participating in a Scenario Planning Extreme project, individuals can leverage the approach to identify three personally meaningful alternative career paths within the
scenarios identified. From there, they can draft corresponding strategies for how
to succeed in each path.

Scenario Planning Extreme Applied to Migration and Integration—In 2015, Europe
experienced a significant influx of asylum seekers, with 1.3 million people arriving, mainly from the Middle East.[122] Of these, 890,000 stayed in Germany[123], creating intense political and social pressure. This event served as the impetus for a
2016 Scenario Planning Extreme seminar focusing on the topic of the EU, migration, and integration in 2040. Chapter 3.2 presents a detailed paper that summa-
rizes the seminar's results. This paper was published in the journal *Acamonta* by
the Technical University Bergakademie Freiberg in the same year, offering insights into how scenario planning can be used to address complex societal challenges.

Chapter 3.2 presents four dramatic scenarios for the future of European society,
alongside several strategies recommended by students who participated in the
seminar.

We include this analysis here because, by 2023, it became evident that the significant influx of refugees into Europe in 2015 was not a one-off, isolated event. Instead, it may have been the harbinger of a "new normal" future for the continent.
This realization is reason enough to reconsider it again today to revisit the

recommendations of students who came from many countries thereby bringing diverse perspectives.

Exploring controversial topics freely—Is the Scenario Planning Extreme approach also suitable to freely explore controversial topics? The answer is yes. In chapter 3.3, we tackle one of the most contentious issues of our time: the global war on psychoactive substances. For over a century, governments have been banning and fighting this issue with decreasing success. To frame this discussion, we refer to the two *Sicario* movies[124] (2015 and 2018), starring Emily Blunt, Benicio del Toro, and Josh Brolin. These movies vividly highlight the violence, tragedy, and unintended consequences of the war on drugs, providing a powerful lens through which to consider the complexities of this ongoing struggle.

Could it be that, in this ongoing battle, the "therapy" has cause far worse effects on our lives over the past decades than the "disease" is seeks to cure? Respected academic criminologists warned us of this as early as 40 years ago[125]. Just raising this question remains, for many, extremely provocative.

Nevertheless, we do it anyway and boldly ask the question: *How can Scenario Planning Extreme help us to find constructive solutions to drug challenges in liberal-democratic societies?* Solutions that both meet people's desire to experience altered states of consciousness and align with and do justice to the long-term interests and well-being of our society?

We recommend using the Scenario Planning Extreme approach to develop a range of scenarios and identify actionable corresponding strategies to bring an end to this absurd, century-long war on psychoactive substances.

3.1
Career Planning
with Extreme Scenarios

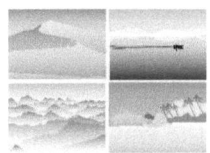

*We must be willing to get rid of
the life we have planned, to have
the life that is waiting for us.*
Joseph Campbell

*I*n the past, it was customary practice for high school students in Germany to have to write a class essay shortly before graduation, reflecting about what they hoped to achieve in life. What career did they dream of? What did they want their future life to look like? Around 1964, Martin listened to a radio drama on Radio Bremen titled The *Class Essay* by Erwin Wickert[126]. Originally written in 1954, the story was already considered an "oldie but goodie" by the time Martin heard it. Told with a backcasting perspective, the drama follows its protagonist hero as he accidentally stumbles across his class's essays thirty years after leaving school. He re-reads them and compares the hopes and dreams of his classmates with the realities of what transpired in their lives.

The radio play poignantly portrays human destinies and the tension between the hopes of the students and the realities they eventually faced in life. All of them ended up living completely different lives from the one they had imagined. Yet, in their own ways, they all coped—sometimes better, sometimes less well—yet ultimately, they each found their place in life and a sense of happiness. All except for

159

one student. He achieved everything he had set out to do. In his essay, he had even accurately predicted the years in which he would achieve them. He married at the exact specified age he had envisioned, became the father of precisely the number of children he had specified, and achieved every one of the career milestones he had described. Yet, after accomplishing it all, took his own life. Everything had turned out exactly the way he had planned but he had reached the end of his dreams. His story blurs the line between a land of milk and honey ... and a vision of hell.

What conclusions can be drawn from this? First, concern for our future affects us all and is universal. Everyone aspires to self-actualize and achieve their dreams, and the typical starting point for us humans is to create plans to get there.

Secondly, life usually gets in the way by rarely unfolding as planned. Along the way, we may encounter unexpected opportunities to apply our talents—opportunities that may turn out to be even more attractive and fulfilling than we had originally hoped. At the same time, it may also turn out that obstacles can arise that prevent us from realizing our plans. We may perhaps lack the necessary tools, resources, or circumstances to successfully move forward on our desired path. Major societal changes can also derail personal aspirations. For many in the 20th century, events such as the two world wars and the rise of totalitarian regimes shattered countless dreams and dashed many personal hopes. Similarly, the consequences of German reunification brought significant upheaval for many in the former GDR. A poignant example of this is the experience of members of Dresden University of Technology, all of whom, after reunification, received letters of dismissal in the mail, accompanied by an opportunity to reapply for their positions at the university.

Thirdly, most people find new paths that they can adapt to, or learn to live with, even thrive in, ultimately discovering their personal happiness. This adaptability is reflected in the statistics on the professions that people transition into after completing their studies, often far removed from their original plans.

Fourthly, the real future lies in embracing ever-new opportunities. Initial career plans should be recognized as provisional directions rather than fixed destinies. One should remain open and be prepared to exchange these plans for better-fitting work-life steps when new possibilities arise.

Finally, clinging rigidly to one's original ideas despite the ever-changing world can be a significant risk, potentially leading to failure. As the radio play so movingly depicts: the classmate who reached all his goals met a tragic end. This reminds us of the importance of flexibility. As sad as this ultimate failure is, it serves as a powerful encouragement to embrace change in our lives, even to seek new opportunities, and be prepared for life's twists and turns. Martin wholeheartedly agrees. His own life turned out to be a case study of this suggestion. It is no surprise that while writing this chapter, he remembered the radio play he heard nearly 60 years ago. Its message remains as relevant now as it was then.

Life's unpredictability teaches us to adapt, evolve, and find new ways to pursue meaning and fulfillment, even when our original plans are disrupted.

As we journey through life with open eyes, we come to recognize that political, economic, social, especially in today's world—technological changes can get in the way or even disrupt our career aspirations. Long- range planning in the face of rapid, unpredictable change presents a paradox: on the one hand, we seek a goal that gives meaning, providing us with purpose and direction, and we plan to figure out how to get there. On the other hand, the fast-paced evolution of the world around us may render that goal obsolete by the time we are prepared for it and ready to pursue it.

Is it worth making plans anyway in the face of this paradox? Our answer is: **Yes!** And: it is not only worthwhile thinking ahead while staying open to changes in the world, exploring them, and trying them on for personal fit with our evolving sense of purpose. If we find alignment and feel comfortable with these changes, we can use them as stepping-stones to explore and try out the next logical sensible step on our path.

Welcome to career planning based on the principles of Design Thinking—a dynamic and iterative approach that emphasizes exploration, adaptation, and continuous improvement as we navigate an ever-changing world.

Careers in Any Future

Bill Burnett and Dave Evans, former managers at Apple and co-developers of the Design Thinking Method, have shown how this approach is ideal for career planning in times of major change—in other words, for all of us. At Stanford University, their seminar on this topic has become one of the most popular courses on campus. Their book, *Designing Your Life*,[127] became an international bestseller, and we recommend it highly.

The two also shared their approach at numerous conferences, including one in Chicago[128]., where they delivered an engaging and inspiring 15-minute presentation. With their dynamic and sympathetic style, they captivated the audience, leaving everyone energized and eager to apply their ideas. We encourage everyone to watch this inspiring speech and witness their enthusiasm firsthand.

This chapter describes the key ideas from their presentation and integrates them with the Scenario Planning Extreme perspective, offering a powerful combination for rethinking career planning and embracing change.

The presentation by the two authors begins with the compelling observation: when it comes to career planning, our own hopes and worries are often joined by errors in thinking, compounded by erroneous assumptions imposed on us by others. They highlight some of the most common misconceptions:

- *"Your studies determine your future". WRONG! Statistics show that within four years of graduation, 75% of students are working outside their field of study. Many assumptions about how clear and linear the career path will be post-graduation simply turn out to be wrong.*
- *"What is your passion?" WRONG! Most of us have multiple passions. In fact, surveys reveal that 85% of people report having several passions. So, the real question is not: which single passion should I follow? But rather, why should I commit to only one?*
- *"At the age of sixteen, you should already know what career you want to pursue". WRONG! Research suggests that we typically only realize which profession truly suits us much later—often between the ages of 30 to 35.*
- *"Do you want to achieve the best possible You?" WRONG! There are not one but several "best versions" of us. There are multiple good versions. CAUTION! The pursuit of an unattainable "best" can become the enemy of an attainable "better"[129] .*

What can a career goal look like? The answer from design thinking is simple: create something meaningful out of your life as you live it. Approach your career by thinking like a product developer—constantly iterating, adapting, and improving. As Joseph Campbell's quote at the beginning of this chapter reminds us, life is not about rigidly following a pre-set path but about embracing the journey and making it your own.

Burnett & Evans succinctly formulate:

"A well-designed life in the sense of design thinking results from recognizing problems and successfully solving them. Step by step. Repeatedly. A secret recipe is to find your own new ways of solving problems and not to follow the ideas and recipes of others." [130]

Think like a designer and

"Distinguish between tame and wicked problems. Tame problems can be solved using known methods. We can calculate how a house must be built to be structurally safe. I can use a navigation device to find the way to my destination - if I am aware that the navigation device shows a map and not the real landscape as we have described it.

It gets wicked when the solutions are only discovered during development. The design criteria are often fuzzy and change over time. This means that we must try them out to recognize whether we have found the solution. This includes the principle of iteration: we try it out, see what is missing, adapt to it, see what is still missing and repeat it until we realize that we have the solution. "[131]

Burnett & Evans open our eyes to the *perspectives of design thinking*. These include:

"Awareness: You only solve problems that you recognize, acknowledge and respect, according to the saying: It is what it is. It takes several years of study to become a physician, no matter how I feel about it.

Empathy: Recognize the actual problem and treat it with childlike curiosity. Be open-minded. See it as an opportunity to discover something completely new. Forget tried and true solutions and the advice of others."[132]

Henry Ford is often quoted as saying: *"The customers would have wanted faster horses."*[133] This highlights the need for visionary thinking that goes beyond conventional expectations. Steve Jobs embodied this mindset with his childlike curiosity and radical openness — two of his most remarkable qualities. At Scenario Planning Extreme, we strive to practice the same inner openness at, embracing and taking an interest in all scenarios, even—and especially—the negative ones.[134] By exploring even the most challenging possibilities, we prepare ourselves to face the future with resilience and creativity.

"Doing is more important than thinking. Trying is better than studying. Build something. Try it out. Improve it. Involve other people as soon as you can. This

way you will benefit from their different perspectives and maps of reality. They can see what you may not recognize." (This reflects a strong kinship with Scenario Planning Extreme, which is conducted in teams and relies on the diverse perspectives of participants, each bringing with them their own unique reality tunnels.) *"Designing your life step* by step *according to the principles of design thinking means doing something, one step at a time. And again, and again.* "135

Burnett & Evans describe five steps of design thinking:

"Define the problem you want to solve.

Positive perspective: See the problem as a positive opportunity.

Design: Find three distinctive designs, each with their own solutions. This opens different possibilities and gives your creativity plenty of scope." 136

Here, too, we recognize a shared similarity in the mindset between Design Thinking and Scenario Planning Extreme: a profound openness to many possibilities.

"Test your designs. Try them out. Learn how you can improve them. Make improvements and try them out again. Repeat this (as with updating and implementing the results of Scenario Planning Extreme).

*Extreme cooperation. Talk to everyone who has something to say on the subject. Talk especially to your distant contacts on the fringes of your personal network. Look for new perspectives in these conversations."*137

Burnett & Evans distill this approach into three short and simple, yet impactful sentences: *'Be interested. Talk to people. Try things out.'*138 With the foundation in place from these preparations, we are now ready to move on to 7practical steps.

Start by Doing Something

We begin by reflecting on our current situation. In the appendix, you will find a proposed questionnaire to help you record your answers. Burnett & Evans recommend starting with a simple but essential step: ask yourself:

"Which 7 to 10 activities are typical for you? How much positive energy do they give you? How useful are they for you? What could you change today? If they

annoy or bore you, what could you do less of today? If they give you joy and meaning, how could you do more of them? Make small, easy-to-implement changes immediately. In this way, you will bring movement into your life.

Talk to others about your ideas. Arouse their interest. Incorporate their thoughts into your own thinking. (This serves as another example of the close relationship between the Design Thinking approach and the Scenario Planning mentality.)

Always remember you have several good selves. You can always strive for a new you. "[139]

Three Prototype Scenario Careers

Next, we visualize three different career options that are both attractive and meaningful to us. By combining Burnett and Evan's method with the insights gained from a Scenario Planning Extreme project—its scenarios and relevant strategies—we create a more comprehensive and forward-thinking approach to career planning.

We deliberately use the term **prototype** for the career, aligning with Martin Gerber's FlowTeam principle of always developing prototypes. This approach helps us to remain aware that our goals can and should evolve as we continue to learn and grow.

To begin, record your ideas on a sheet of paper formatted using the template in the appendix. For each career prototype, consider the following:

Describe **three career prototypes** that are desirable, protect your Siamese Twins (core values and commitments), and give your talents a chance to constantly develop:

- A career in the world as it is today,
- A career in the world of the doubly positive scenario,
- A career in the world of the doubly negative scenario.

For each career prototype, describe its attractiveness to you, as suggested by Burnett & Evans. Reflect on how well it aligns with your values, your talents, and aspirations:[140]

- *"How feasible is it* [within the scenarios] *on a scale of 1 to 100?*
- *Do you have the necessary training?*
- *Do you have the time to acquire the necessary training?*
- *Do you have the skills required for this prototype?*
- *How much do you really like your idea?*
- *How much do you trust yourself?*
- *How well does this lifestyle suit you?*
- *How well does this lifestyle match your values?*
- *How well can you recognize yourself in this job prototype?"*[141]

Do Something

For each of your three career ideas, the following applies:

Role play being an empathetic journalist and visit your three potential futures. Imagine yourself interviewing the "you" who already works in these careers. Think like Positive Deviance: assume that your desired careers already exist out there and seek out examples or individuals who can inspire and inform your journey. Jessica Lippnack and Jeffrey Stamps[142] remind us that your network of contacts is strongest at its edges. If you lack confidence, ask one of your friends to help you. Martin, for example, once asked a distant acquaintance to arrange an interview with a prominent political figure, something he could not have accomplished on his own.

Remember, most people enjoy talking about their work, especially when someone shows a genuine interest in what they do. Burnett & Evans offer some excellent advice to help guide these conversations:

"Don't be afraid of these conversations. It helps if you keep in mind that you and the person you are talking to have a common interest: She wants to tell you what she loves about her work, and you want to hear that from her."[143]

Ask the interviewees about their experiences: How much do they enjoy their life in this role? What gives them a sense of meaning in their work? What frustrates them? What is special about their job? How did they get to their position?

The most valuable approach in these interviews is to adopt the mindset of an empathetic journalist. According to Burnett & Evans, after conducting three to six such conversations, you will have a solid understanding of how well each career aligns with your aspirations. Social relationships thrive on reciprocity. As a gesture of thanks for their time, offer to write a job description based on your conversation and send it to them. Many will see this as fair compensation for the value of their time with you and the insights they shared.

If you feel a mutual connection and sense that you get along well, ask if you can shadow her as an unpaid volunteer for a day. For example, you could assist in simple ways—by taking notes on a flip chart during one of her presentations or by being introduced as a student researching or authoring a paper about her profession. Small opportunities like these provide firsthand experience and deeper insights into your potential career path.

Success is for those who act. Networking is much like a tourist asking for directions in a city—most people are more than happy to help others find their way. Do not be afraid to reach out, connect, and learn from those who have already walked the path you are exploring.

Now, take what you have learned and create short descriptions of your three scenario job prototypes, illustrating what they might look like in practice. Each of the three career prototypes should be about one and a half pages long and address the following key points:

- What is the purpose of this prototype? A short sentence suffices: "*The job does X to achieve Y.*"
- Why is this prototype useful for you? "*When I reach Y, I feel that....*"
- What social contribution does this role make? Two clear, concise sentences. *The shorter, the better.*
- What are the three to five most important tasks in this role? "*I take care of A so that B is achieved.*"

167

- What are two to three key challenges? For example: *"Balancing both F and G is a challenge."* Or: *"Avoiding K while achieving L."*
- Which two or three areas of knowledge and experience are essential for success in this role?

The purpose of this task is to bring your prototypes to life, just as we use storyboards in Scenario Planning Extreme to visualize and evaluate future threats and opportunities. The clearer you can imaginate these roles, the better you can assess their potential fit.

Consider sharing your prototypes with those who helped you and invite their feedback. Their insights could further refine your ideas.

Our goal for this chapter is to demonstrate how readers can prepare for different career scenarios in a variety of quite different future landscapes. Doing this exercise with a trusted friend will significantly enhance its effectiveness. In fact, this kind of mutual career reflection could even evolve into an informal network of scenario career trendsetters, providing ongoing support and fresh perspectives.

Meaningful Scenario Careers at Any Age

Is Scenario Planning Extreme useful for career steps in retirement?

Of course it is. Retirement offers a wealth of opportunities to shape the next phase of life with purpose and fulfillment. It may be worth thinking about exploring three different areas:

(1) Volunteering in social services,

(2) Actively supporting your favorite societal issue—a cause you care about, or

(3) Realizing a lifelong dream.

Of course, these are just a few possibilities—there are countless other ways to make a meaningful difference. The same holds true for people who face barriers to employment or whose access to the world of work is blocked for whatever reasons.

Is it possible to still pursue ambitious goals in retirement? Many years ago, Martin watched a TV report on ESPN2 about an ascent of Mt. Rainier in Washington State.

He was surprised by the presence of an elderly man in the climbing team—someone who clearly found the trek challenging and needed to take frequent breaks to rest. As it turned out, this expedition had been organized specifically for him.

It was James Anderson, who had dreamed of climbing this phenomenal mountain his entire life. At the age of eighty-one, he finally dared to fulfill this dream and make it a reality. When the expedition team finally reached the summit, they were greeted with clear skies and a fantastic breathtaking view. Seizing the moment, the camera crew spontaneously asked James Anderson if he had a message for the world. His message for all of us was simple, yet unforgettable:

Dream big. Dare to fail.[144]

3.2
Extreme Scenarios
about Migration and Integration

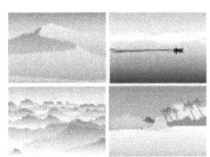

*The values for the desired guiding culture
must come from cultural modernity.*
Bassam Tibi [145]

*S*cenario Planning Extreme seminars with students from around the world offer valuable insights into how policy makers can use this approach to prepare for extreme changes. This chapter reprints an article originally published in 2016 in the journal *Acamonta* of the Technische Universität Bergakademie Freiberg, which is reproduced here with its kind permission.

As Charles Hampden-Turner prepared us in the foreword, reality usually unfolds as a weakened version of one of the extreme scenarios imagined in a scenario project. The more open-minded we are about potential extreme developments—and the better we prepare with appropriate strategies—the easier and more effectively we can navigate to successfully deal with the challenges of even less extreme scenarios.

During these seminars, students—primarily from Mid- and East Asia—developed several suggestions for a range of policy recommendations for Europe that deserve thoughtful consideration. They concern nothing less than the destiny of Europe.

In 2015, over one million refugees from the Middle East arrived in Europe. At the time, this was seen as a temporary crisis. Yet, by2023, it had become increasingly clear that such a large migration might not have been a one-off event. This phenomenon prompts the question: Is it time for more Scenario Planning Extreme seminars to explore the future of migration and integration?

As throughout the book, we continue to use the female form of address in this chapter.

A Long-Term Perspective for Successful Integration in Europe

Ritika Srivastava, Sina Tajik, Jakob Sanders and Martin Gillo
Freiberg University of Mining and Technology, 2016

Abstract: In January 2016, 20 students from eight different nations at the TU Bergakademie Freiberg applied the long-term planning method of scenario planning to answer the question of how the EU can successfully deal with high immigration, especially from Muslim countries, in the long term. The result of this analysis is four possible scenarios and corresponding strategies to achieve the most successful outcome. The most desirable strategies involve strengthening the European economy in combination with the creation of a clear European identity.

Our world is growing ever closer together. People are moving to new places all over the world. The reason for this is globalization, but also the hope for a better life and the flight from wars. Due to the conflicts in the Middle East, the European Union experienced an exceptionally high influx of refugees in 2015. Against this backdrop, many Europeans are asking themselves the question:

How can the EU best harness the benefits of diversification through migration while achieving security, harmony, and prosperity for all in a sustainable way?

A group of international MBA students from the TU Bergakademie Freiberg dealt with this question under the moderation of the fourth author. Using the scenario planning method, various outcomes, and corresponding strategies for the EU were developed.

The Situation in 2015

The EU has experienced an unprecedented development since 2014. In 2015, up to 1.3 million refugees, mostly of Muslim origin, sought a peaceful future in Europe. The large influx of people has presented the EU with challenges that lead to the following questions:

How will immigration affect the EU in the long run? This question is of particular interest to countries such as Germany and Sweden, which have taken in the largest numbers of migrants. How will this level of immigration affect their societies?

What measures can be taken to keep the current situation under control and/or reduce uncertainty? This is an unprecedented situation, which is why suitable solutions must first be developed. This is also one of the main reasons for the enormous uncertainty among the European population.

Thinking about Long-Term Solutions

Is it possible to think about long-term solutions when not even the short-term trends can be predicted? Can predictions be made for the next two, three or five years, or even for the next generation of Europeans? The answer to all these questions is a resounding yes.

The scenario planning approach chosen for this study, i.e., planning with different future scenarios, seems best suited to answering such crucial questions. The methodology was originally developed for the US Army. It was first used in the business world in the 1970s by the Shell Oil Corporation, which used it to gain a major competitive advantage. Since the 1990s, scenario planning has been increasingly used in industry as the preferred tool for long-term planning. A quick look at YouTube shows that well-known universities offer this method as part of their courses.

We are aware that the future is uncertain and often deviates from our forecasts. Scenario planning aims to map the range of all possible scenarios and make them visible by selecting four exemplary outcomes.

In January 2016, a team of 20 MBA students from eight different countries applied the scenario planning method at the TU Bergakademie Freiberg. The aim was to develop various future scenarios for the European Union in 2040 that assume a continued high level of immigration of Muslims. The students were asked to adopt the perspective of advisors to the European Commission.

The first step was to look at potentially relevant developments that are already emerging today. Forward-looking trends are often visible at an early stage but are not considered in terms of their relevance for long-term, future development.

Four Scenarios

The students identified twenty-three different trend groups that they believe could be relevant for the year 2040. Two of these trends were particularly critical. The first predicts a rise in Islamophobia with a concurrent political trend towards the formation of a caliphate in Europe. The second development is characterized by negative economic development combined with increasing social conflicts. Both trends can intensify and weaken. This results in a two-by-two matrix with four scenarios.

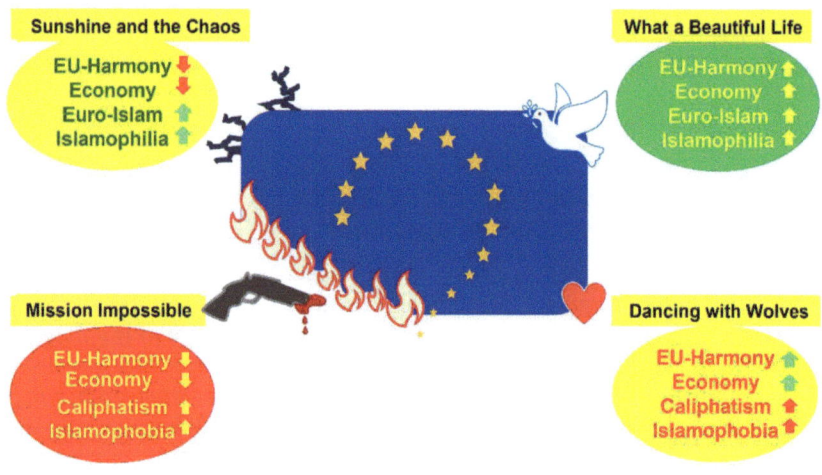

Mission Impossible: *The assumed worst-case scenario with high Islamophobia/caliphate tendencies and negative economic development.*

This prediction follows Murphy's Law: anything that can go wrong will go wrong. In 2040, the European economy will be enormously weakened. The advancing political caliphate tendency on the one hand and Islamophobia on the other have led to social conflicts combined with rising crime rates. The European Union is trying to prevent the collapse of the economy. Within the EU, there is increasing polarization and nationalization of the member states, some of which have already left the Union.

What a beautiful life: *An ideal scenario with low tendencies towards Islamophobia and a caliphate society, accompanied by a strong economy.*

This scenario represents the best possible development. In 2040, everyone is integrated into European society and the economy is booming. New jobs and a better life for more and more people are just some of the benefits of a well-integrated continent. Citizens of different religions, ethnicities and nationalities have learned to live together in peace and harmony.

Dancing with the wolves: *Europe has a strong economy and at the same time pronounced Islamophobia and caliphate tendencies.*

In 2040, there is a robust labor market and a high standard of living for all. Nevertheless, social tensions prevail due to pronounced Islamophobia and the advancing caliphate trend. The influx of migrants has both positive and negative effects. On the one hand, it strengthens the economy; on the other, it leads to social conflict.

Sunshine and the chaos: *A weak economy in Europe, coupled with negligible Islamophobia and caliphate tendencies.*

In 2040, all religions and atheism are respected in Europe. However, the weak economy leads to social conflicts and high unemployment, combined with a rising crime rate. Under these conditions, the influx of refugees places an additional burden on the economy and public budgets.

Strategies to Strengthen European Integration and Identity

What should the European Union do to achieve the best long-term impact of migration under the four scenarios mentioned?

As soon as the various scenarios and their consequences became clear, it became apparent which strategies were most suitable and which minimized the probability of a worst-case scenario occurring. In this way, the students defined 18 "robust" strategies that promise success regardless of the scenario that occurs. In addition, strategies were also developed that are optimally suited to different scenarios.

Six Strategy Options for 2040

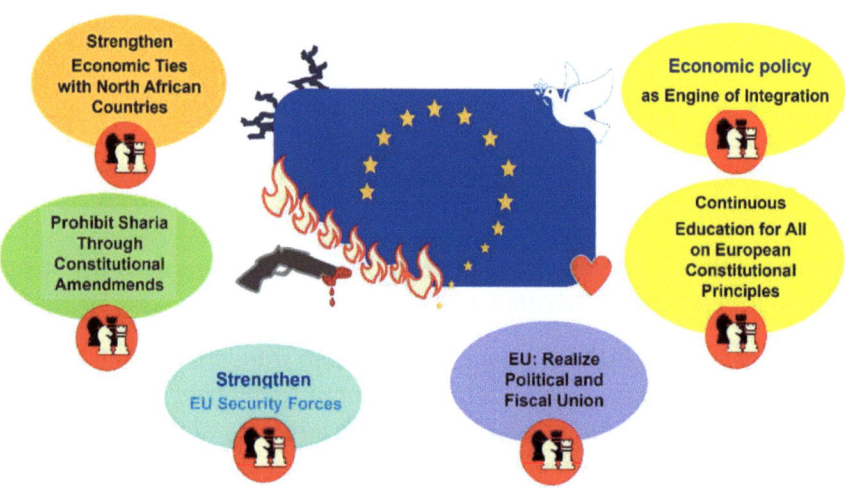

The various strategies were divided into six groups (listed here. The two groups colored yellow were rated as particularly important). *Irrespective of Europe's future development, the focus should be on further strengthening the economy. Prosperity is the basis for peaceful and constructive coexistence. If people can be economically secure and to self-actualize through their work, they will also be more open to new initiatives and ideas.*

On the other hand, social conflicts are exacerbated by economic uncertainty. The fear of unemployment and social decline provides the ideal breeding ground for isolation and aversion to change and innovative ideas.

The second group of strategies concerns the strengthening of European identity, both for those born in the EU and for newcomers. A common understanding of Europe can be promoted by government action - or ignored by its omission.

The strategy proposals for the European Union are:

a- *Strengthening the European economy for the successful social integration of migrant women*

- *Creation of support programs to help highly qualified migrant women to successfully integrate into the labor market.*

- *Incentives for companies:*

    - *promote diversity in their workforce.*

    - *Tax relief for the manufacturing industry.*

    - *Extension of the probationary period upon hire to encourage creating more jobs.*

    - *Temporary suspension of the minimum wage to facilitate the creation of jobs for low-skilled workers.*

- *Preventing the brain drain by investing in infrastructure and future technologies.*

b- *Education to strengthen European identity and commitment to unity in diversity.*

- *Development and implementation of an EU-wide integration program focusing on language, labor market access and acculturation to European values.*

- *Promoting the communication of fundamental European values and European identity*

- *Promoting cultural events for social integration*

- *Communicating values such as respect, tolerance and highlighting the benefits of a diverse society*

- *Promotion of information campaigns on Islamic culture to increase the acceptance of Muslim refugees in the EU.*

- *Strengthening equal rights for people, accompanied by stricter laws to protect women from sexual assault.*

c- *Strengthening the European institutions*

- *Realization of a European political union with a strong constitution*

- *Realization of a European fiscal union.*

d- *Strengthening the European security forces*

- *Doubling of the FRONTEX budget to ensure more efficient organization of refugee flows.*

- *Strengthening security within the EU by creating a uniform information service along the lines of the FBI.*

e- *No to the trend towards a caliphate*

- *Tightening up the European constitution to prevent Sharia law in European legislation.*

f- *Stronger economic cooperation with the Middle East*

- *Strengthening the economy in the Middle East by incentivizing the expansion of economic relations with the EU.*

Summary

This study makes it clear that the EU should do everything in its power to avoid the "Mission Impossible" scenario and make the "Life is Beautiful" scenario more likely. The students agreed that the key to Europe's future lies in promoting European identity through education and strengthening the European economy.

The strategies derived from the scenarios help to integrate qualified refugees into the labor market and thus strengthen the European economy.

Promoting an EU-specific identity is one of the most important steps towards defining fundamental European values. There are currently at least thirty different European identities. What holds them together? The US explicitly defines its culture and identity. The students were convinced that Europe should do the same. Building a strong European identity is an important step towards political union.

Europe's youth should be involved in the formation of a European identity, regardless of their origin. This is a fundamental prerequisite for the vision of an attractive society for all.

Newcomers should be supported by the EU in understanding and respecting European values and learning to appreciate the culture, customs, laws, etc. Their successful integration into society depends on these factors. The EU will also benefit from an intercultural approach.

Every crisis brings opportunities and risks. The students agreed that the EU can minimize its risks and make the most of the opportunities with the proposed strategies.

The teams: Mission impossible: Ehsan Faraji, Maxim Tschulkow, Lee Meng-Chan, Ram Krishna Awasthi, Sridhar Srisuresh. It is a beautiful life: Yasaman Yousefi Ghasemabad, Tess von Branconi, Fatema Darbar, Anh Phuong Nguyen, Hira Javaid. The dance with the wolves: Rajesh Krishnamurty, Sina Tajik, Steban Mendez, Xinbiao Chen, Joseph O. Monye, Ruxing Yao. The sunshine and the chaos: Andres Parra Salazar, Jakob Sanders, Samineh Moghaddas, Ritika Srivastava. Organizational support: Johannes Stephan.

Is Political Reflection
without Blinkers too Dangerous?

A close acquaintance of Martin reacted with great concern after a test reading of this chapter in November 2023, as, from his political point of view ...

> *"... the results that emerged back then are still explosive today. On the one hand because of the fear of Islamization, even caliphate. If interpreted badly, this is an insinuation that does injustice to many Muslims. The Dresden anti-Islamic initiative PEGIDA will see itself confirmed by your authors that there is something to it after all ... I find the perspective with the caliphate tendency and the Muslims very discriminatory and generalizing. There are radical Muslims, yes, but there are so many different great, integrating, educated and enlightened Muslims from different countries of origin. The latter are the majority. It all comes across as very sweeping and abbreviated here. "* [146]

Martin's answer:

"Dear Michael,[147] you are obviously very moved by this topic. Here are a few thoughts on the Scenario Planning Extreme method. The project team deliberately

deals with extreme future scenarios that will hopefully never occur, but for which we should be prepared.

Four extreme scenarios are always selected, both positive and negative. A good extreme scenario planning project is always a provocation ... The extreme scenarios are neither a statement about specific current situations nor a statement about average citizens, regardless of which religion they belong to.

The extremes are deliberately provocative, but in a playful way. ... Only if we are not afraid to confront extreme possibilities can we prepare ourselves accordingly. In doing so, we usually find that there is no need to panic because we can prepare strategies for success that help us to deal with extreme situations. In most cases, the actual future is an attenuated form of extremes. The better we are prepared for them and can cope with them, the better. ISIS has as little to do with average Muslims as Hamas, but Israel must deal with them (after their terrorist attack on Israeli civilians on October 7, 2023), with dire consequences for all Muslims in Gaza.

When analyzing the trends in migration from the Middle East to Europe, two of these trends were seen as particularly risky and dangerous:

- *the issue of economic growth in Europe, as it has a decisive influence on how many people have the chance of a decent life. In a deep recession, people think first and foremost about their own livelihood.*

- *the question of attitudes towards Muslims in our society and the reaction of Muslims to social offers of integration or exclusion. The two are systematically linked.*

This results in four different extreme scenarios. One incredibly positive, one extremely negative, two as a hybrid. The chapter shows which strategies help to avoid the double negative scenario without denying its possibility. The strategies are the right answer, not ignoring challenges.

*In the Scenario Planning Extreme seminars, students present their scenarios and strategies at the end to external, simulated clients ... (*who occasionally try to) *reassure the students: 'You do not need to worry about this double negative possibility. So, your concerned reaction is in good company.*

The ... silence on the topic of migration makes the situation even worse because it leaves this subject of fear to the wrong people and thus inadvertently makes itself complicit in what it is trying to avoid: The rise of xenophobic parties and the simultaneous disintegration of traditional parties. On November 22, 2023, the anti-Islamic Geert Wilders won the elections in the Netherlands.

It is a bit like the question of the risk of fire in houses. If I keep quiet about it, I am not helping anyone but leaving it to those who want to capitalize on people's innate fear of fire and call for a ban on all fires. That would be the wrong answer. The right way to deal with fire hazards is to have a good fire department and fire blankets and fire alarms in every household.

My advice (also) for controversial political issues: Boldly tackle the extremes with scenario planning and find good solutions."

3.3
Alternatives to Drug Bans

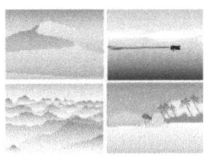

The war on drugs has completely failed.
Barack Obama [148]

*A*ll of us search for meaning in our thoughts and actions. We strive to create something positive out of our lives—not only ourselves, but also for our communities and world at large. This is best achieved when our reality tunnels are aligned closely enough with actual reality so that good intentions lead to satisfactory and sustainable results.

Throughout this book, we have demonstrated how we can use Scenario Planning Extreme. It allows us to playfully explore different futures and their implications, challenge assumptions, and refine our perspectives. By expanding and improving our reality tunnels, we become more open to fresh solutions, co-develop them actively, reach consensus-based decisions, and then implement them with care and courage when the appropriate alert signals arise to warn us.

Challenging restrictive regulations and taboos: This chapter explores how Scenario Planning Extreme can be used to question restrictive regulations and taboos—especially when existing rules cause more harm than they claim to prevent. We will examine two social taboos: one from the past and one from the present.

In the Abrahamic religions of Judaism, Christianity and Islam, same-sex love has historically been—and in some places still is—a taboo. In many periods and regions, it has been forbidden and outlawed under threat of the death penalty. But who is truly harmed when it is practiced between consenting adults?

The religious argument has often been that God forbids it because it would plunge us into social chaos. Who benefited and still benefits from this taboo? History suggests that the real beneficiaries were and continue to be religious and secular rulers. Controlling individual sexuality—particularly through threats of violence against those who deviate from prescribed norms—has granted certain religious elites' significant power and effective control over people in their societies.

The pattern was not limited to religious authorities. The National Socialists (Nazis) in Germany also persecuted and criminalized being gay, sentencing gay men to concentration camps and, in many cases, execution. Even after the fall of the Nazi regime, post-war Western Germany continued to uphold legal restrictions on being gay. For many years, Section 175 of the Western German penal code criminalized same-sex relationships, leading to imprisonment and persecution of thousands.

It was only through a courageous and persistent efforts of the LGBT+ movement in the U.S. and Western Europe that attitudes toward same-sex relationships began to shift—gradually, step-by-step—in the 1970s. Even so, progress was slow. As late as the 2010s, German Chancellor Angela Merkel continued to oppose granting same-sex marriage equal rights to heterosexual marriage, maintaining her stance until the very last days of her sixteen-year tenure in office. Those struggles are now behind us. Today, we can look back and ask ourselves: What were we so afraid of?

Why have we refused for so long not only to accept but to fully recognize same-sex marriage as equal to heterosexual marriage? The answer lies, in part, in the deep-rooted fear of violating religiously prescribed taboos— a feat that still lingers in many societies. Martin recalls that when he was a teenager, his mother worried a bit that he might be gay. It was because of the deeply ingrained cultural and religious norms that made being gay a cause for concern about social acceptance, including her own.

Even today, the fear of coming out may still be overwhelming. A young man in Martin's acquaintance realized as a teenager that he was gay and was so terrified of acknowledging it that he attempted to drive with his car off a cliff instead. His life was saved at the last moment when the front axle broke just before the edge. In the aftermath, he finally gathered the courage to come out to his parents.

Their response? Love, acceptance, and unconditional support, whatever they might or might not have expressed previously.

As a society, too, we feel relieved. Aside from a few remaining critics, we have accepted that same-sex relationships do not endanger our society or threaten our social fabric and should enjoy equal legal status to heterosexual marriage.

We believe that Scenario Planning Extreme could have accelerated the slow process of this gradual shift in perspective. By imagining a society in which same-sex relationships were already normalized, we might have more quickly realized that our attitudes were shaped by external influences rather than personal conviction. It is the willingness and courage to think in extremes that liberates us intellectually, allowing us to explore without fear, situations that once seemed daunting. In doing so, we also expose those who have previously intimidated us. Like the little girl Dorothy in *The Wizard of Oz*[149]—the forces that once dictated our fears and prejudices in our reality tunnels—are unveiled as merely self-constructed. We no longer need to allow them to define and shape our own feelings about consensual behavior among adults.

The Courage to Think about Extremes

Let us address another social taboo: the widespread yet forbidden everyday use of currently illegal psychoactive substances.

The history of the illegalization of psychoactive substances is marked by a quasi-religious zeal, driven primarily by the United States—not only to enforce restrictions domestically on its own population, but to "save" the entire world. This missionary fervor is best exemplified by the American *Women's Christian Temperance Union (WCTU)*[150], whose relentless energetic lobbying efforts even brought about a ten-year ban for all alcohol consumption for citizens in the U.S. through a constitutional amendment. Their ambitions did not stop there; bans on tobacco and other drugs were intended to follow.

Seeking to impose this prohibitionist agenda not only at a national level, but to expand it on a global scale, the U.S., with the active backing from campaigning support of the WCTU and like-minded organizations in Western nations, worked to established worldwide treaties enforcing drug bans. Initially, this effort was pursued through the League of Nations and later institutionalized under the United Nations. In the end, the U.S. succeeded[151] . One of the most significant aspects of such treaties is that they are usually concluded without public debate, allowing sweeping restrictions to take effect without meaningful democratic scrutiny. This lack of discourse has only deepened the entrenchment of prohibitionist policies, despite mounting evidence of their failures.

The development of Morphine, Heroin, and Cocaine in Germany helped thousands of amputee veterans from World War I to lead pain-free lives despite the otherwise chronic pain caused by their injuries. However, the Treaty of Versailles prohibited Germany from continuing to prescribe these drugs, further complicating the lives of those who relied on them.

In 1971, Richard Nixon declared War on Drugs, not only targeting established addictive substances but also adding the then new, non-addictive psychoactive substances—LSD, Mescaline, and certain hallucinogenic mushrooms—to the list of banned drugs. This decision ignored emerging research suggesting that these substances could have therapeutic effects.

Occasionally, the use of psychedelic substances has been reported to facilitate healing experiences. Take, for instance, Martin who initially arrived in the U.S. on a one-year scholarship while engaged to his fiancée. The couple had pledged mutual faithfulness while apart. During the Christmas holiday, they reunited in the U.S. and experimented with a psychedelic substance, likely Mescaline. Under its influence, Martin's fiancée calmly revealed that she was in another intimate relationship. Instead of getting upset, Martin experienced the conversation as if he were watching a movie about himself. Their conversation remained peaceful and understanding, leading both to agree in a calm and friendly fashion to amicably go their own separate ways. A brief time later, Martin was offered the opportunity to continue his studies in the U.S. and seized it.

What was Nixon's true political motive on the War on Drugs? In a 1994 interview with journalist Dan Baum from *Harper's magazine*, Nixon's former White House Counsel, John Ehrlichman, revealed the underlying strategy:

> *"The Nixon campaign of 1968 and the administration that followed had two enemies: the left-wing anti-war activists and the blacks. Do you understand what I am trying to say? We knew we could not outlaw being against the war or being black, but by getting the public to associate the hippies with marijuana and the blacks with heroin and punishing both harshly, we could discredit those groups. We could arrest their leaders, raid their homes, break up their meetings, and thus vilify them night after night on the news. Did we know we were lying about the drugs? Of course we knew that!'* [152]

What were the consequences of such ideological zeal for illegalization? The public responded much the same as they had during alcohol prohibition—they had refused to stop consuming banned substances and instead turned to illegal markets. Just as prohibition in the 1920s fueled the rise of organized crime, so too did the criminalization of drugs. The Mafia, which had grown immensely wealthy from bootlegging alcohol, seamlessly transitioned into the drug trade, cementing its influence in American society, politics, and culture.

By 1929, the U.S. repealed alcohol prohibition, but rather than abandoning its moral crusade, it simply shifted focus—substituting drug criminalization for its former anti-alcohol zeal. In drug policy, "well-intentioned" often proves to be the opposite of "well done". Consider one striking example: The stimulant methamphetamine[153] was first synthesized by a German pharmaceutical company and marketed under the name *Pervitin*. In Germany, it was freely available over the counter and for many years was even incorporated into chocolates as a pick-me-up. Marketed as "housewives' chocolates", it could be considered an early forerunner of today's energy drinks. During this period, there were no known reports of significant fatalities linked to its use. Today, however, methamphetamine is criminalized and traded illegally as crystal meth, with devastating consequences. According to German media reports, crystal meth contributed to over 30,000 deaths in the US alone in 2021[154] . In this case, the effects of prohibition—driven by control and suppression—have proven far worse than the very problem it sought to solve.

What have been the real consequences did this War on Drugs[155] ? So far, the U.S. alone has spent over one trillion dollars on it—with unintended and often counterproductive results. The more the U.S. spends in the drug war, the worse the situation becomes:

- o In 2021, the US recorded over 110,000 drug-related deaths[156]—more than in any previous year.
- o The U.S. also has the highest per capita prison population in the world, with a huge portion serving time for drug offenses.
- o Despite escalating enforcement efforts to suppress them, the drug market for illegal substances continues to grow.

And why?

The answer lies in the economics of addiction. Users must obtain the money to finance their substance consumption, often resorting to theft, robbery, or fencing—where stolen goods are sold for a fraction of their original value. Many also turn to prostitution as a means of survival. A key driver of the market's self-perpetuating growth is that many addicts fund their habit by engaging in drug dealing, actively recruiting new "customers". This also ensures a steady influx of customers, sustaining and expanding the drug economy despite prohibitionist policies.

Beyond the societal impact, it is important to mention there is a deadly risk for the users themselves. Since the use of illegal psychoactive substances is unregulated, users never truly know what substances they are really consuming or in what dosage. Every shot of the drug is a game of Russian roulette—any dose could be fatal. This systemic dysfunction based on the compulsion to play the suicide game affects more than just individuals. Inevitably, society suffers broader consequences when those who disregard themselves do the same to their fellow human beings. When people lose respect for their own lives, they often lose regard for others as well[157] .

Who really benefits from the illegality of drugs? A portion of the profits from the sale of illegal substances is funneled into political influence—often through discreet donations aimed at securing protection, mostly out of public view. What percentage of these proceeds from the illegal trade is used to convince politicians and the law enforcement apparatus to prosecute competitors without getting their own hands dirty, while shielding the paying players? The media has been reporting on such corruption for decades, yet the true extent remains hidden from public view.

One of Martin's acquaintances described that as an East Coast police officer he drew his own personal conclusions. He was occasionally invited to join the anti-drug force units of his police department but steadfastly refused, convinced that doing so, it would come down to the choice between accepting drug money or risking personal accidents. He wanted neither.

Who benefits from prohibition and the resulting illegality of substances?

- The drug cartels, which thrive in an underground economy where high risks mean high rewards.
- The law enforcement agencies, who naturally need to be ever better equipped to fight organized crime, continuously demanding greater resources to fight an ever-expanding drug trade.
- Politicians, who warn of the terrible consequences of drug use and campaign hoping to be re-elected by promising to put an end to drugs, despite their unlikelihood.

The likelihood of successfully eliminating drug use is about the same as enforcing a ban on adultery. Both have been part of human behavior for millennia. The continued failure of drug prohibition raises a disturbing question:

Is this "War on Drugs" turning into a slow-motion suicide of the Western world? Rather than saving society, is it driving it toward self-destruction? Do we have the courage to discuss sensible alternatives openly and specifically?[158]

As we saw in the unjust treatment of Julia Bonk in Chapter 1.4, the topic of drug legalization remains a self-constructed and potent political taboo, capable of threatening and socially ostracizing anyone who dares to question the status quo.

Yet we question it anyway. Not just because it is necessary—but also as a symbolic apology to Julia Bonk and others silenced by this debate.

What Would Be better than a Ban on Drugs?

Who is willing to join a Scenario Planning Extreme project and explore how the future might look with different approaches to drug legislation? Let us engage in a Scenario Planning Extreme exercise to explore this question.

We could imaginate that the United Nations World Health Organization (WHO) invites recommendations on four distinct regulatory frameworks for dealing with psychoactive substances, shaping global policies over the next 25 years. What could life look like in these different scenarios?

Should we also play with a scenario where the possession of just a few grams of drug results in the death penalty, as is currently the case in Singapore? Probably not—such a policy would require constitutional changes in many Western countries, making it an unlikely path.

However, in our Scenario Planning Extreme exercise we can explore more realistic and impactful scenarios, such as:

- o Core Trend 1: The legalization of all psychoactive substances, ranging from semi-legal (partial decriminalization) to comprehensive (full-scale legalization).
- o Core Trend 2: The commercialization of psychoactive substances, transitioning from illegal underground markets to regulated, legitimate industries.

This might result in the following intentionally incomplete scenario matrix, outlining potential futures based on varying degrees of legalization and commercialization. Would you like to work in a team to refine the details of these scenarios and construct a more complete scenario matrix to analyze their potential outcomes?

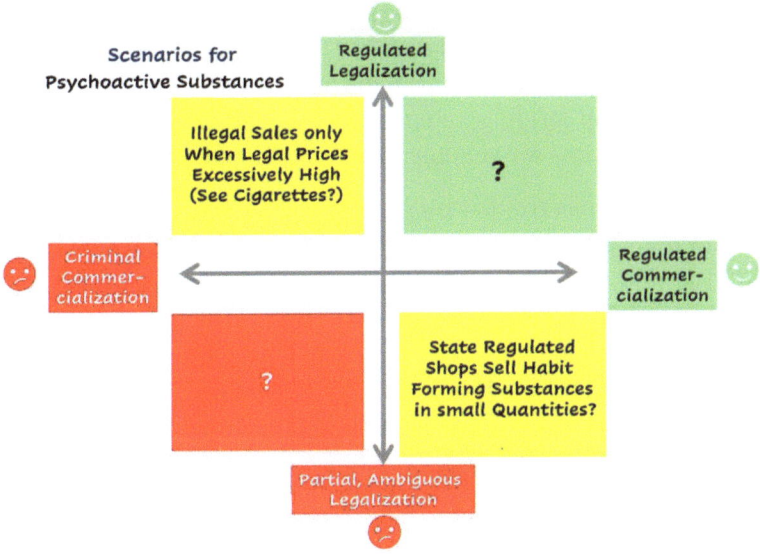

Scenarios for
Psychoactive Substances

Regulated
Legalization

Illegal Sales only
When Legal Prices
Excessively High
(See Cigarettes?)

?

Criminal
Commer-
cialization

Regulated
Commer-
cialization

?

State Regulated
Shops Sell Habit
Forming Substances
in small Quantities?

Partial, Ambiguous
Legalization

Thinking Beyond Taboos:
A Call for Scenario Planning Extreme

We should develop our own adaptive and transformative strategies for each of these scenarios, exploring how we can live constructively within them. Through this process, we could playfully and critically assess what is truly in our best interest—as a society, as a community, and as individuals.

We could also examine what forms of legislation or regulatory exemption from drug laws with what new rules of the game—analogous to existing frameworks for the regulation of tobacco, alcohol, and over-the-counter pharmaceuticals—would best serve our long-term well-being. Just as crucially, we need to determine what level of legal regulation is compatible with a free and democratic basic order, which taboos we must overcome, and how to best realize meaningful reform.

For over forty years, leading criminologists in academia have been calling for an end to the criminalization of drug use—yet their voices have been stubbornly ignored. Most of the causes of death from illegal substances are unintentional overdose, substance impurities, and unknown adulteration with deadly substances. All three are the direct consequences of illegality.

We believe that Scenario Planning Extreme can make an important contribution to this complex debate. Let us take off our ideological blinders, explore a range of different extreme scenarios for the full legalization of psychoactive substances, and develop careful strategies to design our way towards judicious implementation. The time for genuine open-mindedness is long overdue.

Addressing the genuine issues—treatment and systemic reform: Any viable strategies within the various scenarios must also tackle the reality of drug addiction. Classic drug addicts—whose ability to choose freely is often compromised— should be considered as patients in need of treatment, not criminals. The current refusal to provide adequate medical care and legal pathways for these individuals condemns them to lead a dead-end existence, from which they can only escape by death—and, before that, a life of desperation resulting in personal conduct without compassion for others.[159]

Beware of half-measures: Tempted to go for half-hearted legalization? Watch out! A half-hearted approach to legalization is not a real solution. Consider, for example, a policy that legalizes only the possession of small personal-use quantities of drugs while keeping large-scale trade illegal. Such a move would guarantee that drug trafficking remains in the hands of organized crime, maintaining the very dangers we seek to eliminate. Only if we are prepared to imagine a broad spectrum of different extreme scenarios will we be able to discover and embrace systemic, well-structured, constructive, and sustainable solutions that truly serve the long-term interests both of our society and our citizens.

Fearless reflection on other controversial topics

Why not try out the logic of Scenario Planning Extreme to think through controversial issues with a few friends? Thinking through difficult topics can help us confront deep-seated fears, challenge assumptions, and uncover unexpected opportunities. Here are some questions to get you started:

- What is our topic of fear?
- What exactly concerns us about it?
- Let us imagine that this fear becomes reality in the next 25 years. What could our lives look like then?
- What constructive ideas do we have to successfully deal with this scenario?

- What hidden opportunities might emerge?
- How can we proactively prepare for this possibility?
- Who could support us in this effort?
- How could we tell when our fear scenario is becoming reality? What early warning signs would indicate that it is unfolding and what action is needed to address it?

If Scenario Planning Extreme can be of significant help to break through stubborn political taboos, imagine how much easier it would be for us to practice training our minds to become open to extreme changes in everyday life. By adjusting our reality tunnels, we will come closer to reality. With more open eyes we gain a broader and clearer perspective on the world around us than we would otherwise be able to see.

We conclude with encouragement: Let us all embrace the many possible opportunities life offers—and have the courage to take advantage of them, pursuing even solutions which seem initially unconventional. The future belongs to those willing to go beyond their fears.

3.4
Succeed Together
in Every Future

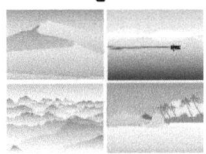

What you must do,
do it playfully.
Joseph Campbell [160]

*M*artin once presented a new personnel concept to AMD executive committee member Tony, who, as was his habit subjected him to a stress test on him— a challenge he posed to anyone presenting innovative ideas. After scrutinizing the proposal, Tony found no flaws and, with a hint of frustration, grumbled: *"Why are you only making this proposal now?"*[161] Martin smiled and replied: *"Tony, that question is the hallmark of all good ideas."* Tony laughed—and gave his full support to Martin's proposal.

We are convinced that Scenario Planning Extreme is precisely that kind of powerful and overdue idea—one so promising that we must ask ourselves: Why we are only now taking it seriously, adopting it, and using it to our advantage. Let us explore the key benefits of applying Scenario Planning Extreme:

Scenario Planning Extreme: **A method for everyone.** Originally, designed for experts, Scenario Planning Extreme gained traction thanks to the credibility of its early adopters in strategic thinking. Herman Kahn, a key figure in the U.S. defense community, helped establish its legitimacy, while scenario planning experts at Shell, —including Arie de Geus, Peter Schwartz[162] and Charles Hampden-

195

Turner—further developed and popularized the approach. Today, however, it is no longer limited to specialists. The method now thrives on the broad participation of individuals with diverse perspectives, or what we call different reality tunnels. Each person's reality tunnel represents only a fragment of the broader true reality landscape. Our Siamese Twins—the rational and emotional sides of our thinking—limit our perspective and do not allow a holistic understanding. But when we bring together people with vastly different reality tunnels, their diverse worldviews increase our ability to see beyond our personal limitations on the meaning of life. We then have a greater chance of approaching a more comprehensive view of the landscape of reality—one that would be inaccessible to any single individual.

Planning as learning. At its core, learning is about testing ideas—subjecting them to stress testing until we determine that they are solid and prove robust enough to withstand stress tests, much like Tony's approach in the example above. This process allows tactics to evolve into strategies, step by step, in the same way that Steve Jobs and his team refined their innovations. It is important to note that Scenario Planning Extreme is not about predicting the future. It is about learning to imaginate possible futures, learning how to succeed in them, and growing beyond our current limitations.

Learning together through play. We practice Scenario Planning Extreme in a safe, protective, and stimulating learning environment, sometimes in seminars, other times at weekend learning conferences. By approaching complex topics playfully, we bypass our defense mechanisms, which might otherwise block us from considering divergent perspectives. In this space, we are free to (and should) explore a wide range of possibilities, examining their potential implications and effects on the key question being considered. What if? Scenario Planning Extreme thrives on and welcomes curiosity and inquiry of this kind. We use a variety of brainstorming techniques to generate and evaluate ideas. Every perspective is welcomed—whether it comes from an individual with a unique insight or reflects a broad group consensus, all are taken equally seriously. The process fosters open-minded exploration, allowing us to challenge assumptions and expand our collective understanding.

Mastering the future. No one can predict the future that will become reality. But we can imagine multiple possible futures, each offering valuable insights into what might unfold. This is the intellectual jewel and power of Scenario Planning Extreme—a method that helps us analyze different possible futures, giving us

196

insight into what may become reality, recognize opportunities, and anticipate threats. By looking at and engaging with different futures, we also gain clarity to recognize our options and confidence to take advantage of the opportunities, navigate challenges, and develop strategies to avoid or minimize threatening situations. This process empowers us with the courage to do what confirms and affirms our purpose in life. Aligned with our purpose while also cultivating the serenity to accept things that we cannot change, Scenario Planning Extreme becomes a liberating tool for coping with and shaping the future. Instead of passively reacting to change, we take an active role—focusing on what we can change, we co-create our own path forward to our future.

Extremes make you fearless. The playful exploration of extreme scenarios might seem like an oxymoron. Shouldn't we be afraid of them? Surprisingly, we are not. The emotionally liberating power of extreme scenarios lies in the fact that their likelihood of occurring is irrelevant, playing no role at all. In a learning environment, we engage with each scenario as playfully and curiously as we might examine an unexpected object found on a weekend hike through a forest. Through this process, we playfully experiment with strategies that could lead us to success—even in the most extreme conditions. And if reality later turns out to be a weakened, less intense version of an extreme scenario, then the strategies we have prepared can still be applied in a modified form, strengthen resilience and enhancing future viability for individuals and organizations alike.

Alternatives liberate us from deadlocked stagnant thinking. Scenario Planning Extreme has a deeply liberating effect—it helps us recognize, embrace, and act on the fact that there are multiple options in all situations. By expanding our perspective, we uncover hidden opportunities, anticipate, and avoid potential threats, and become ever more successful. This mindset applies not only to organizations but also to each of us as individuals. The practice of continuously seeking alternatives becomes a habit, instilling courage, and strategic adaptability. Simply realizing that there are multiple paths forward—even when we feel trapped— empowers us to act, transforming what once seemed like dead ends without alternatives into new possibilities.

Breaking free of quantitative blinkers. The true potential of Scenario Planning Extreme lies in its independence from past assumptions and its openness to exponential change—shifts in the future that often defy traditional quantitative analysis. Rather than being limited by the constraints of historical trends, this approach focuses on long-term development potential, allowing us to anticipate and adapt to fundamental changes in the rules of success. By adopting this perspective, participants gain the ability to recognize the early signs of important innovations and black swans —transformative events that may already be emerging in an "infant stage." This method frees both intellect and emotion, encouraging us to use our own imagination and creativity in shaping the future.

Playfully protecting our Siamese Twins. Through Scenario Planning Extreme we embrace a form of "heart learning", as described by Johann Pestalozzi—an approach that fosters deep, experiential understanding. This process helps us to recognize that every potential future can be good for us—to see the potential opportunities and empower us to imaginate our role in shaping them. By intentionally colliding with our reality tunnels with extreme scenarios and success strategies, we expand our mental flexibility and discover new possibilities. Since this exploration is done in a playful way, our emotional watchdogs—our natural defense mechanisms—remain at ease, allowing us to think freely and creatively without fear or resistance.

Changing behavior together. Scenario Planning Extreme builds on Kurt Lewin's groundbreaking insights into behavioral change. Old habits and convictions are most effectively "unfrozen" when done collectively in an environment among equals. When a group acknowledges the shortcomings of past behaviors together, the transition to new insights, behaviors, and norms becomes much easier to achieve. This collective approach is also invaluable for the subsequent successful implementation of the newly agreed behaviors. A group that evolves together, united in this way, naturally develops its own sense of group loyalty, which protects its members from external pressure and attempts to revert to old habits and outdated convictions. In this way, Scenario Planning Extreme strengthens long-term change by fostering a supportive and resilient community.

Scenario Planning Extreme is **an excellent watchdog.** It acts as an early-warning system for the future. We focus on identifying scenario alert signals—key indicators that serve as harbingers of the future change. By detecting these signals early, we position ourselves to be the first to implement our carefully prepared strategies for the future when a specific corresponding scenario begins to unfold. The scenario alert signals help us to keep an eye on possible futures. Since no organization can pursue, finance, or staff every strategy at once, it is crucial to only act when the scenario is recognizable as clearly emerging. Scenario alert signals serve as guiding beacons. After the corresponding signal lights up, we then track possible futures and ensure that we deploy the right strategies at the right time.

Prepare early. A strategic shift is much like steering a massive tanker to change course at sea—it takes a lot of time, foresight, and careful planning. Developing a new strategy requires significant organizational, financial, and personnel adjustments, all of which need to be mapped out in advance. The is where Scenario Planning Extreme provides a decisive advantage. By preparing for extreme scenarios ahead of time, we ensure that when change becomes necessary, we are ready to act swiftly and effectively rather than scrambling to react.

Recognizing wolves in sheep's clothing. Participants in Scenario Planning Extreme learn to identify trends in the present that have the potential to become serious threats in the future. This sharpens their ability to recognize or develop an eye for the possible exponential growth potential of certain developments in everyday life. Even trends that may seem harmless today can bear significant risks, eventually turning out to be wolves. With this experience, they gain from such projects, navigating everyday life with greater awareness, spotting hidden dangers before they escalate.

Recognize sheep in wolf's clothing. The same applies the other way round. Some trends that initially appear threatening may harbor groundbreaking opportunities—containing the seeds of great innovation hidden beneath their current "wolf's clothing". Recognizing the potential for innovation within perceived threats requires a bit of courage and open-mindedness. But for those willing to look deeper, it can be very worthwhile to look at their positive potential (even beyond the task of scenario planning). These can lead to transformative breakthroughs, both in scenario planning and everyday decision-making.

Competitive advantage for pioneers. We live in a world of perpetual competition. Shell is convinced: "In the future, our only competitive advantage will be to learn faster than our competitors." Scenario Planning Extreme is one way to accelerate an organization's speed of learning—through adaptation and innovation. The larger the internal supporter base for this approach, the more employees become attuned to new emerging opportunities and threats—and the more proactive they become in developing solutions on how to successfully deal with them. Encouraging employees to actively contribute their ideas fosters an innovative, driven culture, making the organization more agile, forward thinking, and resilient in the face of uncertainty.

The power of fans. Steve Jobs was one of the first to recognize the positive game-changing influence a passionate fan base has on the success of corporate strategies. Inspired by his approach, it is worthwhile considering:

- o Which external trendsetters are willing to support and promote this strategy in public?
- o How can we find them, engage them, and network them into a dedicated fan base?

Building a community of advocates can be a critical preparatory activity for scenario-based strategies—particularly those requiring public acceptance to succeed.

Get vaccinated today. Vaccinations are an effective and affordable way to protect against serious diseases. Consider Scenario Planning Extreme as a mental vaccination—a safeguard against being caught off guard and blindsided by extreme changes. Those who prepare in advance will be the first to adapt, seize opportunities, and thrive when the unexpected becomes reality.

Organizations seen as HuLiOs. We view organizations as living entities—Human-Like Organizations (HuLiOs). Like human beings, they possess:

- o Their own self-image that shapes their identity,
- o A purpose that defines their mission,
- o Core values they stand by and guide their decisions.

Scenario Planning Extreme strengthens this organizational identity, helping businesses to further enhance their reality tunnels and align their strategies with evolving futures. By embracing this approach, organizations refine their adaptability to succeed in all possible futures, strengthen themselves, and ensure that they continue to develop their potential and thrive despite growing and intensifying competition and uncertainty.

Good for society at large. Commercial enterprises do not exist in a societal vacuum. Instead of operating in isolation they are deeply embedded in society. They serve people, create jobs, and contribute to the well-being of their communities. Their profits are taxed, their employees' incomes are also taxed, and these solidarity contributions fund essential pillars of society, including social welfare programs, education and research, cultural institutions, and many other national and international commitments. This is the foundation of a functioning market economy—and the engine of prosperity. When businesses thrive, employment rises, everyone is doing well, economies grow, and even the most vulnerable members of society, including the needy, benefit.

We humbly hope that a widespread adoption and broad use of Scenario Planning Extreme can also make a small but meaningful contribution to maintaining and strengthening both organizations and our society at large—ensuring resilience, innovation, and sustainable success, whatever the future may bring.

Scenario Planning Extreme as **personal mentor.** We invite our readers to cultivate an attitude of radical openness—embracing the potential opportunities hidden in extreme futures. By adopting Scenario Planning Extreme as a form of personal mentor, you can apply its principles not just to organizations, but to your personal life.

This mindset expands your vision, helping you recognize unexpected possibilities and approach life with a lifelong learning perspective. More importantly, it instills the courage to act–to experiment, adapt, and seize opportunities that might have otherwise gone unnoticed.

Embracing this approach transforms uncertainty from something to fear into something to explore—a personal tool for growth, resilience, and success in an ever-changing world.

Open your eyes to new opportunities with this lifelong learning perspective and have the courage to try it out!

Attachments:

Example of a scenario storyboard

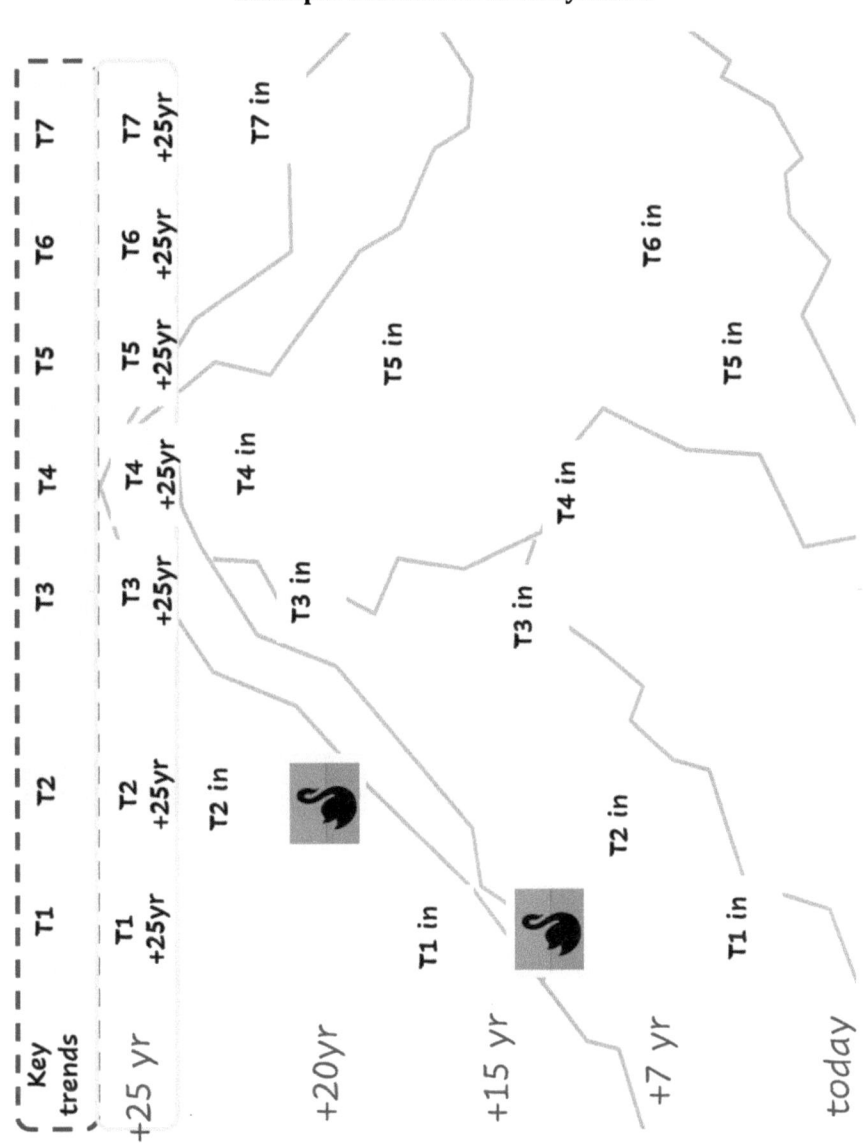

Two templates for personal scenario planning

Draw these templates on a sheet of paper and fill them out:

MY CURRENT ACTIVITIES					
7-10 THINGS I DO RIGHT NOW	POSITIVE ENERGY Rate 0-10	Why and how does it make me come alive?	NEGATIVE ENERGY Rate 0-10	What I dislike about it?	ACTION: What can I do more of?	ACTION: What can I do less of?

3 DIFFERENT PROTOTYPE LIVES		Prototype 1:		Prototype 2:		Prototype 3:	
Questions	0-100	...because:		0-100	...because:		0-100	...because:
1. Do I have the resources for realizing that particular self? Do I have the training? Do I have the time? Do I have what it takes?							
2. How much do I like it? How hot on it am I? How cold on it am I?							
3. How confident am I to pull it off?							
4. COHERENCE: Is this possible life really ME? Is it coherent with who I am? With MY values? Can I see myself doing it?							

Prototype Job Title

_____

Purpose (1):

Personal Meaning (1):

Contribution to Society (2):

Prototype Job Tasks (3-5):

Job Challenges (2-3):

Knowledge and Experience needed (2-3):

Selected Literature

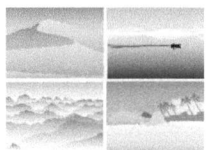

Aurelius, Marcus: **Meditations.** Penguin Classics, London, 2006.

Bogdanich, Walt and Forsythe, Michael: **When McKinsey Comes to Town**. The Hidden Influence of the World's Most Powerful Consulting Firm. Random House, New York, 2022.

Burnett, Bill and Evans, Dave: **Designing Your Life:** How to Build a Well-Lived, Joyful Life. Knopf, New York. 2016.

Collins, James C., and Porras, Jerry I.: **Built to Last**: Successful Habits of Visionary Companies. Harper Collins, New York, 1994.

Csikszentmihalyi, Mihaly: **Flow:** The Psychology of Optimal Experience (Harper Perennial Modern Classics), New York, 2008.

De Geus, Arie: **The Living Organization**. Growth, learning and longevity in organizations. Nicolas Brealey Publishing, London, 1997.

Gardner, John W.: **Self-Renewal:** The Individual and the Innovative Society. W. W. Norton and Co, New York, 1995.

Grove, Andrew S.: **Only the Paranoid Survive**. How to Exploit the Crisis Points That Challenge Every Organization and Career. Doubleday, New York, 1996.

Guderian, Heinz: **Achtung Panzer!** The Development of Tank Warfare (W&N Military) (English Edition), Weidenfeld & Nicolson, Amazon Kindle Edition, New York, 2012. The original was published in Germany in 1918.

Hampden-Turner, Charles: **Maps of the Mind**. Charts and concepts of the mind and its labyrinths. Macmillan Publishing Company, New York, 1981.

Hampden-Turner, Charles: **Ideas from the Edge.** A life in paradox. The Institute of Leadership, London, 2023.

Kahane, Adam (2011): **Transformative Scenario Planning.** Working Together to Change the Future. Berrett-Koehler Publishers Inc, Oakland, CA, 2011.

Kahane, Adam (2017): **Collaborating with the Enemy**. How to work with People You Don't Agree with or Like or Trust. Berrett-Koehler Publishers Inc, Oakland CA, 2017.

Kahneman, Daniel: **Thinking, Fast and Slow.** Penguin Publishing, London, 2016.

Klein, Naomi (2021): **The Shock Strategy**. The Rise of Disaster Capitalism. Hoffman and Campe Verlag GmbH, Munich. 2021.

Kübler-Ross, Elisabeth (2008): **On Death and Dying:** What the Dying Can Teach Doctors, Nurses, Clergy and Their Own Families, Routledge, London, 2008.

Lippnack, Jessica and Stamps, Jeffrey (1993): **The TeamNet Factor.** Bringing the Power of Boundary Crossing into the Heart of Your Business. Oliver Wright Publications, Inc, Essex Junction, VT, 1993.

Manns, Mary Lynn, and Rising, Linda: **Fearless Change:** Patterns for Introducing New Ideas, ResearchGate.Net, 2005. https://www.researchgate.net/publication/200773301_Fearless_Change_Patterns_for_Introducing_New_Ideas

Metzinger, Thomas: **The Ego Tunnel**. A New Philosophy of the Self: From Brain Research to the Ethics of Consciousness. Piper Verlag, Munich, 2021.

Niebuhr, Reinhold: **The Moral Man and the Immoral Society:** A Study in Ethics and Politics. Westminster John Knox Press, Louisville, KY, 2021.

Osbone, Diane K.: **A Joseph Campbell Companion**. Reflections on the Art of Living. Harper Collins Publishers, New York, 1991.

Pasquale, Richard, Sternin, Jerry and Sternin, Monique: **The Power of Positive Deviance:** How Unlikely Innovators Solve the World's Toughest Problems. Harvard Business Press, Brighton, Massachusetts, 2010.

Popper, Karl: **The Open Society and Its Enemies.** Routledge, Oxfordshire, 2011.

Schwartz, Peter: **The Art of Foresight**. Planning for the Future in an Uncertain World. Doubleday Currency, New York, 1991.

Senge, Peter M.: **The Fifth Discipline**. The Art and Practice of the Learning Organization. Doubleday Currency, New York, 1990.

Suleyman, Mustafa with Bhaskar, Michael: **The Coming Wave**. Technology, Power and the 21st Century's Greatest Dilemma. Crown Publishing Group, New York, 2023.

Taleb, Nicolas Nassim: **The Black Swan**. The Power of Highly Improbable Events. Pantheon Verlag, Munich, 2018.

Watzlawick, Paul: **The Invented Reality**. How Do We Know What We Think We Know? Contributions to Constructivism. W. W. Norton & Company, New York 1984.

Watzlawick, Paul: **The Situation is Hopeless but Not Serious.** The Pursuit of Unhappiness. Norton and Company, New York, 1993.

Acknowledgements

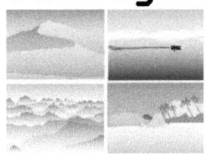

*All that is not given
is lost.*
Rabindranath Tagore

$\mathcal{T}$he ingenious approach of scenario planning has inspired me for over thirty years. In 2004, as Saxony's State Minister for Economic Affairs and Labor, I was able to apply this approach in a pilot project: "Saxony 2025: Options for a strong future". Leading personalities from business, science, culture, media, diplomacy and many volunteers from the Saxon Ministry of Economic Affairs and Labor were involved. Charles Hampden-Turner, one of the pioneers of scenario planning at Shell, was on hand to guide us. The knowledge gained from this experience and the subsequent years of conducting scenario planning seminars along with including new thinking such as "Black Swans" led to Scenario Planning Extreme.

Horst Brezinski, Chair in Economics at the TU Bergakademie Freiberg, and I started offering seminars on scenario planning for students from all over the world in 2007. We were actively supported by Johannes Stefan and Tom Teubner. Working with interested students with this method was always a welcome challenge and a pleasure at the same time. Many thanks to both. Horst and I also brought Scenario Planning to the University of Economics in Poznan. Alexey Nechaev invited me to present Scenario Planning twice at the University of Samaria in Russia. A big thank you for this opportunity, combined with the hope for peace throughout Europe sooner than later, which will make such cooperation possible again in the future.

Edeltraut Günther, Chair of Environmental Economics at TU Dresden, invited me in 2017 to begin holding seminars on scenario planning there. Her successor, Remmer Sassen, continues to provide those seminars with key resources. I was supported in the seminars at TU Dresden by Stefan Lueddeckens, Coco Klußmann and Robert Petri as partners.

Ute Enderlein and I have been teaching scenario planning at the Saxony Hochschule für Verwaltung in Meissen since 2019, where we teach this concept to future decision-makers in the Saxony State administration. Ute has significantly improved this manuscript with good suggestions.

Anyone breaking new ground can benefit from the support and encouragement of friends. For Scenario Planning Extreme, so far these have been Friedbert Damm, Katrin Dunker, Michael Eßlinger, Niels-Christian Fritsche, Inka Hocke-Klotsche, Torsten Holmer, Andre Koberg, Herbert Lappe, Bernd Saupe, Jutta Schmidt, Frank Schwarz, Frank and Friederike Warkus, and Mike Wolff.

Karen Bruggeln and Jochen Grabler from Radio Bremen helped me to rediscover the moving radio play "Der Klassenaufsatz", [The Class Essay], by Erwin Wickert, with which chapter 3.1 begins.

The original version of this book was written in German. Translating a book calls for the support of a native speaker. For this book it was Linda O'Riordan. I cannot overstate my appreciation for the help she provided me, not just for her support with the right tone of conversation but also with helpful content questions and suggestions along the way. This is not to hide the support from the contributions from the worldwide volunteers at Wikipedia, from Programs like Microsoft Office, Co-Pilot, and DEEPL.

Finally: My special thanks to Annette, my partner for over 35 years, who supports and encourages me always, including my ventures into the field of organizational philosophy, like this book.

Martin Gillo
Dresden, 2025

Index

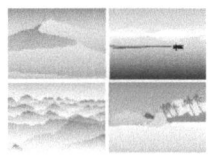

1

1926ers · 33
1926ing · 29, 30, 31, 33, 34, 37, 45, 100

3

3M Corporation · 94

A

Amazon · 29, 105, 147
AMD · 29, 45, 61, 63, 72, 73, 74, 101,
    106, 137
Anderson, James · 122
Anderson, Wes · 88
Android Operating System · 95, 110
Android Operating System · 30, 31
Apple · 30, 31, 95, 100, 110, 117
ASCI Red Computer · 29
AT&T · 28, 29, 30, 31, 40, 108, 110
Autonomous taxi cabs · 100
Autotelic · 63, 64

B

Backcasting · 89, 90
Bezos, Jeff · 105
BioNTech · 94
Black Swan · 111, 148, 154
Black Swans · 20, 37, 90, 149
Blunt, Emily · 114
BMW · 28
Bogdanich, Walt · 45, 146
Bonk, Julia · 49, 134
Brolin, Josh · 114
Burnett, Bill · 6, 117, 118, 119, 120, 121,
    146
Busch, Wilhelm · 112
BYD · 37

C

Campbell, Joseph · 43, 116, 118, 137,
    147
Change · 40, 93, 103, 111, 147
ChatGPT · 38, 111
Chicago · 117
China · 34
Chinese astrology · 31
Cisco · 29

Climate change · 33, 95
Cocaine · 132
Collins, James · 43
Cologne Cathedral · 56
Colombia · 69
COVID-19 · 69
Csikszentmihalyi, Myhaly · 61, 62, 63

D

Danzig · 32
DARPA Defense Advanced Research
  Projects Agency · 96, 111
Darwin, Charles · 78

E

Early adopters · 101
Ehrlichman, John · 132
Eisenstein, Sergei · 88
European Union · 34, 37, 48, 73, 76, 77,
  95, 97, 102, 103, 113, 123, 124, 125,
  126, 127, 128
Evans, Dave · 6, 117, 118, 119, 120, 121,
  146

F

Finland · 30
First World War · 33
Flow · 61, 62, 64, 147
FlowTeam Dynamics · 61, 63, 64, 92
Floyd, George · 38
Ford, Henry · 67, 118
Forer, Bertrand · 31
Forsythe, Michael · 45, 146
Fortune Business Magazine · 43
France · 33
Freiberg, TU Berga · 86

G

Galileo Galilei · 78
Gardner, John W. · 27, 52, 54, 147
Gerber, Martin · 61, 63, 92, 120
German Chancellor · 49, 95, 130
Germany · 1, 6, 21, 28, 33, 34, 35, 37,
  41, 44, 50, 95, 113, 116, 124, 130,
  132, 133, 147
Geus, Arie de · 44, 45, 47, 71, 109, 111,
  112, 137, 147
Global English · 68
Google · 29, 30, 38, 95, 101
Great Britain · 33, 68
Group Dynamics · 53, 61, 62, 63, 67
Grove, Andrew (Andy) · 40, 41, 147
Guderian, Heinz · 33, 147

H

Hallucinogenic mushrooms · 132
Hampden-Turner, Charles · 35, 51, 123,
  137, 147, 149
Hegel, Georg Friederich Wilhelm · 32
Heroin · 132
Hewlett Packard · 43
Holbrook, Anthony (Tony) · 137
Hudson Institute · 18, 35
HuLiO · 15, 44, 45, 46, 47, 52, 72, 108

I

IBM · 18, 28, 29, 39, 45, 108, 110
Intel · 29, 40, 45, 96, 110
International School in Geneva · 69
iPhone · 30, 31, 95, 97, 108, 110
iPhones · 94
Israel · 18, 32, 35, 129

J

Jobs, Steve · 30, 94, 97, 100, 118, 137, 139
Judaism, Christianity, and Islam · 32

K

Kahane, Adam · 69, 147
Kahn, Herman · 35, 36, 137
Kübler-Ross, Elisabeth · 45, 46, 147

L

Las Vegas agreement · 79
Leary, Timothy · 26, 55
LGBTQ+ · 130
LSD · 132
Lucas, George · 88

M

Mafia · 132
Mario M. · 50
Matsushita · 56
McKinsey · 30, 45, 146
Media Lab at MIT · 61, 67
Mencken, Henry Louis · 97
Mental maps · 16, 26, 28, 55, 57
Mental Models · 53, 55, 57
Merkel, Angela · 130
Meroni, Giuliano · 61
Mescaline · 132
Methamphetamine · 133
Metzinger, Thomas · 26, 147, 154
Microsoft · 29, 38, 110, 150
Montessori, Maria · 102, 104
Moore, Gordon · 40
Moore's Law · 40
Morphine · 132

MP3 · 94
Musk, Elon · 101
Muslims in Gaza · 129

N

Nicknames · 86
Nicknames for trends · 81, 86
Niebuhr, Reinhold · 93, 147
Nixon, Richard · 21, 132
Nokia · 28, 29, 30, 31, 40, 108, 110
Non-Government Organizations · 43, 44, 51
Norway · 95, 97
NVIDIA · 101

O

Obama, Barack · 130
OPEC · 18, 35, 36, 37, 100

P

Pasquale, Richard · 97, 147
Perennial skeptics · 16, 101
Personal Mastery · 53, 54
Pestalozzi, Johann Heinrich · 87, 138
Plato · 24
Porras, Jerry · 43, 146
Positive Deviance · 97
Prussia · 32, 33
Prussian General Staff · 33, 34
Psychedelic substances · 132

R

Reality tunnel · 16, 21, 26, 27, 28, 32, 33, 37, 38, 39, 44, 46, 52, 55, 57, 61, 67, 69, 72, 87, 99, 100, 105, 109, 119, 130, 131, 136, 137, 138, 140

Re-freeze · 103

S

Samsung · 38, 95
Sanders, Walter Jeremia III (Jerry) · 45
Scenario funnel · 36
Schmidt, Helmut · 95, 149
Schwartz, Peter · 137, 148
Senge, Peter M. · 52, 53, 54, 55, 56, 57, 58, 59, 148
Shared Vision · 53, 56
Shell · 18, 19, 35, 36, 43, 44, 47, 100, 109, 111, 124, 137, 139, 149
Siamese Twins · 16, 27, 33, 34, 87, 99, 100, 104, 106, 109, 137, 138
Sicario movies · 114
South Africa · 69
Soviet Union · 18, 35
Star Wars · 108
State of Saxony · 50
Sternin, Jerry and Monique · 98, 147
Sweden · 124
Systems Thinking · 53

T

Tagore, Rabindranath · 149
Taiwan · 41, 96
Taleb, Nassim Nicholas · 37, 148, 154
Team Learning · 53, 57
Thunberg, Greta · 33, 38
Tibi, Bassam · 123
Toro, Benicio Del · 114
Treaty of Versailles · 132
Trend followers · 101
Trendsetters · 101
Truman, Harry R. · 99, 100
TSMC · 96
TÜV · 44

U

U.S. President · 49
Unfreeze · 16, 103
United Nations · 131, 134
US Prohibition of Alcohol · 132, 133, 134
USA · 1, 18, 21, 28, 29, 31, 32, 33, 35, 38, 96, 110, 124, 133

V

Vietnam · 98
VUCA world · 18
VW, Volkswagen AG · 96

W

War on drugs · 21, 114, 130
Watzlawick, Paul · 26, 40, 148, 154
WCTU · 131
Western astrology · 32
WHO · 134
Wickert, Erwin · 116, 149
Wilson, Woodrow · 33
Winvick, Stan · 106

X

Xerox · 43, 110

Y

Yes And · 40, 108

References Used
plus Some Personal Notes

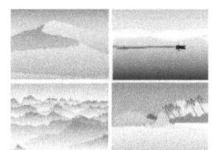

*I*n comparison with traditional scientific methods of planning and organizing, scenario planning is a "street urchin" and should stay that way. This applies to Scenario Planning Extreme: the art of imagining, exploring and learning about potential future opportunities and risks that are so extreme that they provoke in us emotional rejection, i.e., the contrast effect. Its strictly qualitative imagining approach is closer to the art of painting than to the scientific study of the genome. Any attempts to academicize it risks taking away its power to anticipate. Tying scenario planning projects to quantification methods of trends beyond a three- to five-year time horizon, such as through in industry standard seems to me like trying to create an industry standard for creating a great painting.

Ideally, Scenario Planning Extreme will always be a mixture of imagining and rigorous logical exploration. The references in this book are therefore a mixture of academic sources, internet publications and human communication.

The books cited also appear in the "Selected literature" section. As you might expect, most of the sources cited were authored in English. References to the Internet are as of October 23, 2023, unless otherwise stated.

As of 2024, most internet search engines provide an automatic translation service for foreign language entries. Therefore, the several German language internet sources quoted in this book should be no barrier to our English language readers.

[1] Suleyman, Mustafa with Bhaskar, Michael: **The Coming Wave**. Technology, Power and the 21st Century's Greatest Dilemma. Crown Publishing Group, New York, 2023. The authors use numerous examples to describe the fundamental changes that artificial intelligence and synthetic biology will trigger in our world now right now and not just in the distant future. They highlight the positive and negative potential. Particularly threatening is the questioning of the primacy of nation states, which are the basis of all solidarity systems: "In the next 10 years, AI will be the greatest force multiplier in history. It could enable a redistribution of power on a historic scale.". Page 210.

[2] Taleb, Nicolas Nassim: **The Black Swan**. The power of highly improbable events. Pantheon Verlag, Munich, 2018. The book opens our eyes to the importance of improbabilities in our society.

[3] Soros, George: https://de.wikipedia.org/wiki/George_Soros.

[4] Watzlawick, Paul: **The Invented Reality**. How do we know what we think we know? Contributions to constructivism. Piper und Co. Verlag, Munich, 1981 (see also selected literature). Watzlawick was a prominent figure in radical constructivism, a beacon of its principles. His speeches were transformative events that everyone wanted to attend. He died in Palo Alto, California, before I had the opportunity to meet him in person. Watzlawick advocated convincingly that we are not able to see reality with our own eyes. We only see what we have constructed ourselves. This makes him one of the early pioneers of the thinking in brain research and authors such as Thomas Metzinger.

[5] Metzinger, Thomas: **The Ego Tunnel**. A New Philosophy of the Self: From Brain Research to the Ethics of Consciousness. Piper Verlag, Munich, 2021. p. 45: "The experience of being outside your own brain and not in a tunnel (is) generated by neuronal systems deep inside the brain." (see also selected literature)

[6] https://en.wikipedia.org/wiki/Reality_tunnel

[7] Gardner, John W.: **Self-Renewal: The** Individual and the Innovative Society. W. W. Norton and Co., New York, 1995. Gardner was a cabinet member in Lyndon B. Johnson's administration and campaigned for equal opportunities. He subsequently founded the civil rights movement Common Cause, which enforced far-reaching information rights for citizens. He was also a lecturer at Stanford University until his death. His themes were: meaningful lifelong self-renewal. He lived it himself. A remarkable man and a remarkable book.

[8] Gardner, John W.: The **Meaning of Life** https://jamesclear.com/great-speeches/personal-renewal-by-john-w-gardner. John Gardner's definition of the meaning of life, which we use in this book, forms the conclusion of this speech from 1990, which is well worth reading.

[9] "Navigation device does not distinguish between bridge and ferry" (2010): https://www.swissinfo.ch/ger/alle-news-in-kuerze/navigationsgeraet-unterscheidet-nicht-zwischen-faehre-und-bruecke/8264594

[10] IBM https://de.wikipedia.org/wiki/IBM One of the most successful companies in the world that, like all learning organizations, makes mistakes and admits them.

[11] https://en.wikipedia.org/wiki/IBM

[12] Personal communication Stan Winvick.

[13] Intel Corporation. https://de.wikipedia.org/wiki/Intel Today's world of PCs and parallel supercomputers would be inconceivable without this pioneer of the semiconductor industry. This also includes single-minded toughness vis-a-vis its stakeholders.

[14] The supercomputer ASCI Red. https://de.wikipedia.org/wiki/ASCI_Red reports on the history of the development of massively parallel computers based on interconnected Intel microprocessors. "The first application was the collaboration between Intel and the Caltech California Institute of Technology in the Concurrent Computation Project in the mid-1980s, in which 64 Intel 8086/8087 processors were interconnected. This was followed by the Intel Paragon parallel computer and finally, in 1996, the ASCI Red supercomputer built by Intel and installed at Sandia National Laboratories, which was the fastest in the world until the end of the 2000s.

[15] https://www.youtube.com/watch?v=CEcsy8b2hVo&list=WL&index=21 How is it that IBM still exists at all?

[16] AT&T https://de.wikipedia.org/wiki/AT&T

[17] On October 24, 2023, investigative humorist John Oliver dedicated an entire show to McKinsey's controversial practices in his HBO series and on the YouTube channel: https://www.youtube.com/watch?v=AiOUojVd6xQ with examples of the organization's questionable morals. In it, he also refers to McKinsey's prediction of a global market for cell phones of 900,000 units.

[18] Nokia https://de.wikipedia.org/wiki/Nokia The history of this successful organization shows a high degree of openness to new opportunities. Its early focus on the newly emerging cell phone industry brought it to the top with a global market share of over 50 % in 2007. However, it also shows the danger especially for the most successful companies to underestimate innovative ideas from the competition for too long.

[19] Jobs, Steve (2005): **Speech at Stanford University Graduation 2005** ENGLISH SPEECH | STEVE JOBS: Stanford Speech (English Subtitles) – YouTube: https://www.youtube.com/watch?v=UF8uR6Z6KLc. Steve Jobs goes straight to the heart of the students - and our own.

[20] iPhone: https://de.wikipedia.org/wiki/IPhone The iPhone revolutionized the world like no other product in 2007.

[21] Theconversation.com, 2017: **Nokia had the best smartphone in the world - then came the "inferior" iPhone.** https://theconversation.com/nokia-had-the-worlds-best-smartphone-then-came-the-inferior-iphone-70958 January 6, 2017.

[22] Bertrand. R. Forer: *The fallacy of personal validation: A classroom demonstration of gullibility.* In: *Journal of Abnormal and Social Psychology.* Band 44, 1949, S. 118–123

[23] Personal communication Waldemar Gillo.

[24] Greta Thunberg: https://exxpress.at/festhalten-laut-greta-thunberg-bleiben-noch-drei-monate-bis-zum-klima-kollaps/ and https://exxpress.at/doch-keine-klima-apokalypse-greta-thunberg-loescht-duestere-vorhersage-fuer-juni-2023/ Bing also confirms this information.

[25] Guderian, Heinz: **Attention Panzer.** Traugott Bautz Verlag GmbH, Nordhausen (see also selected literature). In 1918, Guderian became internationally known with this book. The American General George C. Patton is said to have exclaimed after a successful tank battle against the Wehrmacht: "Guderian, I've read your book". By tracing

many battles of the First World War, the book describes how the tank as a strategic weapon came into being, was ignored by the German military by "1926ing" and were the root of the total disaster for German warfare in 1918. The book documents that the urban legend of "stab-in-the-back" was a diversionary maneuver by the German military to keep from being blamed for their strategic failure. It was not the home front that led to Germany's failure, but the wishful thinking of the military, who repeatedly talked down the danger posed by the enemy's new armored weapon: 1926ing, i.e. wishful thinking in its purest form.

[26] China is the world champion in automobile exports: https://www.dw.com/de/studie-chinas-autobauer-werden-export-weltmeister/a-66102074

[27] See afterword by Charles Hampden Turner.

[28] Herman Kahn: https://de.wikipedia.org/wiki/Herman_Kahn

[29] De Geus, Arie: **The Living Organization**. Growth, learning and longevity in companies. Nicolas Brealey Publishing, London, 1997. The book is a classic. Despite many awards, it has received less attention than Senge's book "The Fifth Discipline". This book is an asset to anyone who reads it.

[30] OPEC: https://de.wikipedia.org/wiki/Organisation_erd%C3%B6lexportieren-der_L%C3%A4nder

[31] Personal communication Charles Hampden-Turner.

[32] Personal communication Charles Hampden-Turner.

[33] The scenario technique. https://de.wikipedia.org/wiki/Szenariotechnik. A glance at this page shows that the German-language combination of trend analysis and scenario perspective can easily lead to project participants putting on quantitative blinkers that prevent them from considering extreme changes in the environment relevant to the organization. The scenario funnel illustrates this dangerous self-restriction.

[34] Taleb, Nicolas Nassim: **The Black Swan**. The power of highly improbable events. Pantheon Verlag, Munich, 2018 (see also selected literature). The book opens our eyes to the importance of improbabilities in our society.

[35] Greta Thunberg: https://de.wikipedia.org/wiki/Greta_Thunberg

[36] George Floyd: https://de.wikipedia.org/wiki/T%C3%B6tung_von_George_Floyd#George_Floyd

[37] Chat GPT: https://de.wikipedia.org/wiki/ChatGPT

[38] Personal experiment.

[39] Watzlawick, Paul: **The Situation Is Hopeless but not Serious.** Watzlawick's constructivist approach is also at the heart of strategic therapy. The therapeutic solution means prescribing exactly the symptom that the patient is complaining about. If an overweight patient comes to the therapist and asks for help to lose weight, the strategic therapist may prescribe that she first put on a few kilos. It doesn't help a pessimist to hear reasons for optimism. Rather, it helps her to paint an even bleaker picture of the future, one that is too black for her, and motivates her to look for signs that will help her develop a more positive outlook. The book is an example of this kind of spiritual healing.

[40] Personal communication Kent Liebman.

[41] Grove, Andrew S.: **Only the Paranoid Survive**. How to Exploit the Crisis Points That Challenge Every Organization and Career. Doubleday, New York, 1996. The book lives

from its fantastic title. Andy Grove was not only an effective top manager at Intel, but also a highly successful author who wrote regularly for the San Jose Mercury News. His positive external reputation was not always shared by the organization's employees.

[42] Personal communication Georg Milbradt.

[43] Osbone, Diane K.: **A Joseph Campbell Companion**. Reflections on the Art of Living. Harper Collins Publishers, New York, 1991. p. 24. Joseph Campbell became famous in the US as a consultant for the "Star Wars" film trilogy. This book by Diane Osborn reads like a collection of aphorisms with wisdoms from all cultures of the world.

[44] Senge, Peter M.: **The Fifth Discipline**. The Art and Practice of the Learning Organization. Doubleday Currency, New York, 1990.

[45] Collins, James C. and Porras, Jerry I.: **Built to Last**: Successful Habits of Visionary Companies. Harper Collins, New York, 1994 This book is one of a series of books from the 1980s and 1990s that have been passed on as role models in the business world. Time has not been kind to them, as some ten years after publication many of the role models have fallen from the pedestals on which they were placed by the various authors. Our insight from this is that the continuity of an organization's success depends on how the bosses see themselves: If they see themselves as governors and relay runners in a generational succession, they will act accordingly. This works best if they have been promoted from within their own ranks. This minimizes the risk of a mentality that focuses on short-term success at all costs.

[46] Senge, Peter M.: 1990, p. 17.

[47] De Geus, Arie: **The Living Organization**. Growth, learning and longevity in organizations. Nicolas Brealey Publishing, London, 1997.

[48] Technischer Überwachungsverein TÜV https://de.wikipedia.org/wiki/T%C3%9CV

[49] De Geus, Arie: pp. 12-14.

[50] De Geus, Arie: https://hbr.org/2016/03/learning-to-learn#:~:text=It%20forces%20them%20to%20understand%20and%20react%20quickly,%E2%80%9Dcould%20be%20the%20only%20sustainable%20competitive%20advantage. p. 188.

[51] De Geus, Arie: p. 18.

[52] Bogdanich, Walt and Forsythe, Michael: **When McKinsey Comes to Town**. The Hidden Influence of the World's Most Powerful Consulting Firm. Random House, New York, 2022. We are familiar with the book's argumentation from various reviews but have not read it ourselves. A look at McKinsey's Wikipedia page also confirms the controversial reputation of the successful organization. On October 24, 2023, humorist John Oliver dedicated an entire show from the HBO series "Last Week with John Oliver" on the YouTube channel to McKinsey's questionable practices: https://www.youtube.com/watch?v=AiOUojVd6xQ with examples of the organization's questionable ethics.

[53] Bogdanich and Forsythe: ibid.

[54] Advanced Micro Devices Inc. (AMD): https://de.wikipedia.org/wiki/AMD. From 1980 to 2002, I was employed at AMD, serving in various roles, including Director of Human Resources in Sunnyvale (Silicon Valley), Geneva, and Dresden. Beginning in

1995, I also held the position of Managing Director at AMD Saxony Manufacturing GmbH in Dresden.

[55] Kübler-Ross, Elisabeth (2008): **On Death and Dying:** What the Dying Have to Teach Doctors, Nurses, Clergy and Their Own Families, Routledge, London, 2008. See also https://de.wikipedia.org/wiki/Elisabeth_K%C3%BCbler-Ross. She was the first to describe the five stages of dying. Since then, the usefulness of this concept has been demonstrated in many other fundamental changes.

[56] De Geus, Arie: Ibid.

[57] Kahneman, Daniel: **Thinking Fast and Slow.** Penguin Verlag, London, 2016. See also the interview with Daniel Kahneman on Swiss television https://www.youtube.com/watch?v=_fPdSEnLxvg

[58] In his Gettysburg address, Abraham Lincoln characterized democracy as government "of the people, by the people and for the people". This means that taken together as a group of all voters, the voters are always right – of course within the limits of our constitution's boundaries. By implication this calls for **radical empathy with** and **attribution of dignity** to even those, whose opinions I may despise as much as they may despise mine. There is no alternative if we want to live together in harmony and peace.

[59] Julia Bonk proposes the legalization of marijuana and heroin: https://de.wikipedia.org/wiki/Julia_Bonk

[60] My opinion.

[61] **Mario M. on the roof of the prison:** https://www.bild.de/regional/dresden/jva/mederake-klettert-erneut-auf-knastdach-38575966.bild.html This incident rendered the two-years of work of the government commission on demographic development in Saxony worthless in the media.

[62] Personal communication Charles Hampden Turner.

[63] Gardner, John W.: **The Meaning of Life** https://jamesclear.com/great-speeches/personal-renewal-by-john-w-gardner

[64] Senge, Peter M.: **The Fifth Discipline**. The Art and Practice of the Learning Organization. Doubleday Currency, New York, 1990. The author has hit the bull's eye with this book, even if it is difficult reading. Especially in times of rapid change, learning is becoming the most important quality for mastering the future. Our references to his book all refer to the original American edition from 1990.

[65] Ibid, pp. 6-10.

[66] Ibid, Chapter 10, p. 174 ff.

[67] Ibid, Chapter 9, p. 139 ff.

[68] John W. Gardner: Personal Renewal.

[69] Senge, Peter M. 1990, Chapter 10, p. 174 ff.

[70] Personal communication Eckhard Ruhrmann.

[71] Senge, Peter M., 1990, Chapter 11, p. 205 ff.

[72] Ibid. Chapter 12, p. 233 ff.

[73] Ibid. S. 9.

[74] Kahneman, Daniel: **Thinking, Fast and Slow**. Farrar, Straus and Giroux, New York, 2013. The author received the Nobel Prize for this breakthrough contribution to our thinking about thinking.

[75] Ibid., Chapter 13ff., p. 273 ff.

[76] Ibid, p. 281.

[77] Ibid, p. 287.

[78] Ibid, p. 341.

[79] Ibid. S 300.

[80] Giuliano Meroni in his role as AMD's Head of Marketing and Sales for Europe https://www.forevermissed.com/gmeroni/about on January 18, 2024

[81] Group dynamics. See https://de.wikipedia.org/wiki/Gruppendynamik. We humans are social beings. "We define ourselves by our own individuality and our membership in various social groups. We also define our meaning through our belonging and our contributions to communities of solidarity. Group dynamics is concerned with how we can work together constructively in groups and enrich each other through our different perspectives, for the benefit of our communities of solidarity."

[82] Csikszentmihalyi, Mihaly: **Flow: The Classic Work on How to Achieve Happiness: The Psychology of Happiness.** Rider Penguin, New York, 2002. An important book that is well worth the effort of reading.

[83] Gerber, Martin: **FlowTeam Dynamics.** Some geniuses avoid writing conventional books - to the detriment of us all. Such is the case with Martin Gerber of FlowTeam Dynamics. We reproduce here a minimalist website from the organization that graphically illustrates some of his 12 FlowTeam principles. http://www.flow-team.com/doc/FlowTeamApproach_0.84.pdf. AMD Europe has benefited greatly from his advice over the years. His ideas are now being passed on by his successors.

[84] https://www.frontiersin.org/articles/10.3389/fpsyg.2022.989572/full

[85] Kahane, Adam: **Transformative Scenario Planning.** Working Together to Change the Future. Berrett-Koehler Publishers Inc, Oakland, CA, 2011 The author shows how scenario planning can bring and keep divided parties together by envisioning different futures and developing innovative ideas.

[86] Kahane, Adam: **Collaborating With the Enemy**. How to work with people you don't agree with, don't like, or don't trust. Berrett-Koehler Publishers Inc, Oakland CA, 2017 In this book, the author goes even further. Even the title: "Collaborating with the Enemy" is a successful provocation, because this is the worst accusation you can make against someone in a hostile conflict. In this book, Kahane convinces us that peace is often only possible if we are prepared to think about a peace with our worst enemies that everyone can live with, including our enemies. How controversial can that be? Who in the EU dared to say out loud during the Ukraine/Russia war that both sides should talk with each other to stop the killing of young men on both sides of the fronts?

[87] Metzinger, Thomas: **The Ego Tunnel**. A new philosophy of the self: From brain research to the ethics of consciousness. Piper Verlag, Munich, 2021 (also see selected literature). Our brains are made up of many separate minds, but how do they manage

to present themselves to us as one identity? The author answers this question in this fascinating and thought-provoking paperback. he also looks at artificial intelligence.

[88] De Geus, Arie: **The Living Organization**. Growth, learning and longevity in organizations. Nicholas Brealey Publishing, London, 1999, pp. 100-111. De Geus refers to the concept of personalism of the psychologist William Stern: Person und Sache, Zweiter Band: Die menschliche Persönlichkeit, 2nd edition Leipzig: Verlag von Johann Ambrosius Barth, 1919, pp. 6, 9, 40ff.

[89] Advanced Micro Devices Inc. https://de.wikipedia.org/wiki/AMD

[90] Personal communication Stan Winvick.

[91] Jerry Sanders is the charismatic organization founder and long-time CEO of AMD Inc. https://en.wikipedia.org/wiki/Jerry_Sanders_(businessman) on January 18, 2024

[92] EU goals and values: https://european-union.europa.eu/principles-countries-history/principles-and-values/aims-and-values_de The five values described are almost identical to the values of a European guiding culture proposed by Bassam Tibi. What still seems to be missing from the EU values is the principle of the participation of citizens in political decisions at EU level. The EU is probably still on its way to becoming a HuLiO in the sense of our book. As of 2024, the EU appears to be more committed to various special interest groups than the voters.

[93] The following trend wall was created as part of the Scenario Planning Extreme seminar entitled: "2048: Scenarios for personnel management in public administration".

[94] Why are the scenarios "only" differentiated based on the two main trends and four scenarios? For pragmatic reasons: Four scenarios are easy to remember, and clear scenario wake-up signals can be found for them. Three main trends would result in 2x2x2=8 scenarios. In practice, it has been shown time and again that concentrating on two to four scenarios makes the most sense in organizations.

[95] Proverb, American: see Osbone, Diane K. p. 26.

[96] https://de.wikipedia.org/wiki/Panzerkreuzer_Potemkin

[97] https://www.starwars.com/

[98] https://de.wikipedia.org/wiki/Asteroid_City

[99] Personal communication Martin Gerber.

[100] Niebuhr, Reinhold: **The Moral Man and the Immoral Society:** A Study in Ethics and Politics. Westminster John Knox Press, Louisville, KY, 2021. The son of German immigrants, he became the most respected theologian in the US. His most famous statement is nowadays associated with the Alcoholics Anonymous movement.

[101] Personal communication Waldemar Gillo.

[102] BioNTech https://de.wikipedia.org/wiki/Biontech

[103] 3M Minnesota Mining and Manufacturing Organization https://de.wikipedia.org/wiki/3M

[104] Personal conversation.

[105] DARPA: https://de.wikipedia.org/wiki/Defense_Advanced_Research_Projects_Agency

[106] Autonomous cabs in US cities: https://www.axios.com/2023/08/29/cities-testing-self-driving-driverless-taxis-robotaxi-waymo

[107] SEMATECH https://gaz.wiki/wiki/de/SEMATECH on 16.11.2023

[108] Promotion of the Intel factory in Magdeburg. https://www.zdf.de/nachrichten/politik/intel-staatsmittel-subvention-chip-fabrik-magdeburg-100.html

[109] Financed investments by TSMC in the US https://www.heise.de/news/TSMC-Chipfertigung-in-den-US-Firmenvorstand-genehmigt-Milliardeninvestition-4954361.html

[110] https://en.wikipedia.org/wiki/Positive_deviance

[111] Pasquale, Richard, Sternin, Jerry and Sternin, Monique: **The Power of Positive Deviance**: How Unlikely Innovators Solve the World's Toughest Problems. Harvard Business Press, Brighton, Massachusetts, 2010. This remarkable book describes eight major societal challenges and how they could be overcome with positive deviants and their creative ideas. From overcoming hunger in Vietnam to preventing female mutilation practices to successfully combating resistant deadly germs in hospitals, Positive Deviance has repeatedly proven to be an effective solution where other approaches have failed.

[112] Ibid, chapter 2.

[113] Truman, Harry R.: https://de.wikipedia.org/wiki/Harry_R._Truman How to ignore all warnings of disaster and go down with it. He was buried by the landslide and ash from the Mt. St. Helen volcano in Oregon, US.

[114] Comment by Linda O'Riordan: While working on this English translation of the original version, the recent example of the Los Angeles wildfires in January 2025 come to mind. Like Harry Truman, some individuals chose to stay behind to protect their properties from looters or for other personal reasons. According to reports from The New York Post (January 10[th & 18th], 2025) and the Wall Street Journal (January 15th, 2025), approximately 80 residents in neighborhoods including Altadena and Pacific Palisades defied evacuation orders and chose to remain in their homes. This decision led to several tragic outcomes, underscoring the ongoing relevance of Mr. Truman's fate from the early 1980's.

[115] This view of social change is very similar to the **Diffusion of Innovation Theory**, a well-known and widely used sociological framework which explains how new ideas, technologies, products, or behaviors spread within a social system over time. Developed by Everett Rogers in his 1962 book Diffusion of Innovations, the theory identifies key factors influencing the adoption of innovations and categorizes individuals based on their willingness and speed to adopt. The theory's components include the innovation itself, communication channels, time, and the social system (group, individuals, or networks) in which the innovation spreads. Rogers identified five categories of adopters based on their willingness and speed to adopt an innovation, equivalent to this illustration moving from right to left: **Innovators (2.5%); Early Adopters (13.5%); Early Majority (34%) Late Majority (34%)** and **Laggards (16%)**. Because we found the caravan metaphor with slightly rounded figures and "normal distributionized" symmetry as Everett Rogers did to be a useful communication tool without wanting in any way to relativize Everett Rogers' pioneering and precise research results.

[116] Lewin, Kurt: https://de.wikipedia.org/wiki/Kurt_Lewin discovered how people change their beliefs in a group. He called this three-stage process unfreezing, changing, freezing.

[117] Jeff Bezos' three rules for productive meetings (thinkbusiness.ie)

[118] Stan Winvick was AMD's very diplomatic Chief Human Resources Officer from 1980 to 2003: https://www.geni.com/people/Stanley-Winvick/6000000181734903827 on January 18, 2024.

[119] It is worth noting that this approach is most effective when all groups are aligned in their interest to work collaboratively towards achieving a positive overall outcome. However, in situations where politics or competitive dynamics might create resistance or intentional blocking, it may not always be advisable to openly share the intended actions with everyone. In such cases, the level of transparency should be carefully fine-tuned and thoughtfully considered to ensure the strategy remains effective without unintentionally creating additional challenges.

[120] Manns, Mary Lynn, and Rising, Linda: **Fearless Change:** Patterns for Introducing New Ideas, ResearchGate.Net, 2002. https://www.researchgate.net/publication/200773301_Fearless_Change_Patterns_for_Introducing_New_Ideas

[121] New York Stock Exchange - Wikipedia

[122] https://commission.europa.eu/strategy-and-policy/priorities-2019-2024/promoting-our-european-way-life/statistics-migration-europe_de

[123] BAMF - Federal Office for Migration and Refugees - Publications - Migration Report 2015

[124] Sicario movies: https://de.wikipedia.org/wiki/Sicario_ (2015)

[125] I recall that in the 1980s, the German weekly magazine *DIE ZEIT* published an article in which some respected university criminologists analyzed the vicious spiral of the ever-growing drug market and argued for comprehensive legalization as a solution. Unfortunately, —though not surprisingly—their insights were ignored at the time. Given the ongoing urgency of this issue, republishing this article could make a valuable contribution to today's debate. Perhaps now is the time to finally take it seriously.

[126] Wickert, Erwin: **The Class Essay**. A radio play from 1954, re-edited by Sebastian Tippe 2005. https://www.youtube.com/watch?v=3Lt_S5H9G04&t=21s.

[127] Burnett, Bill and Evans, Dave: **Designing Your Life:** How to Build a Well-Lived, Joyful Life. Knopf, New York. 2016. A highly practical book that guides readers to become aware of their own talents and interests, think about multiple future possibilities, explore them through trial and error, and discover meaningful next steps in their professional lives.

[128] Burnett, Bill and Evans, Dave, 2017: https://www.youtube.com/watch?v=1Na-gjMv2Y4&t=197s. In just over fifteen minutes, the two authors successfully manage to convey and communicate their ideas to participants at a conference in Chicago, delivering a compelling and impactful presentation.

[129] Ibid.

[130] Burnett & Evans 2017 ibid.

[131] Ibid.

[132] Ibid.

[133] Ibid.
[134] Ibid.
[135] Ibid.
[136] Ibid.
[137] Ibid.
[138] Ibid.
[139] Ibid.
[140] Ibid.
[141] Ibid.
[142] Lippnack, Jessica and Stamps, Jeffrey: *The TeamNet Factor: Bringing the Power of Boundary Crossing into the Heart of Your Business.* (Oliver Wright Publications, Inc, Essex Junction, VT, 1993). Although a classic, its ideas have proven to be spot on. As social media continues to shape our interactions, keeping these principles in mind becomes even more valuable for successful networking.
[143] Ibid.
[144] At 81 years old, James Anderson successfully climbed Mt. Rainier with a team, demonstrating extraordinary perseverance and determination. While unfortunately, no direct video reference is available, the event has been confirmed by Bing. Martin happened to watch a film report on ESPN 2, which made a strong impression. He will never forget the quote at the end of the report. In the original English version, James Anderson offered us this powerful advice: "Dream big. Dare to fail."
[145] Tibi, Bassam: https://beruhmte-zitate.de/zitate/137317-bassam-tibi-die-werte-fur-die-erwunschte-leitkultur-mussen-der/. Bassam Tibi has long been a sought-after social scientist, who dedicated himself to addressing the challenges of integration. Among his many contributions, we owe him thanks for identifying the **five core values of the European cultural concord: democracy, secularism, enlightenment, human rights, and civil society.** Unfortunately, his important work was later distorted in socio-political discourse when Germany's conservative CDU party attempted to co-opt his ideas to advocate for a national culture standard and exploit it for political gain with popularist slogans including "children instead of Indians".
[146] Personal exchange in conversation with a good friend.
[147] Name changed.
[148] Obama, Barack: https://www.reuters.com/article/us-column-debusmann-drugs-idUSBRE83F0ZR20120416
[149] The Wizard of Oz: https://de.wikipedia.org/wiki/Der_Zauberer_von_Oz
[150] Women's Christian Temperance Union W.C.T.U.: https://www.wctu.org/issues "*The WCTU believes in self-control, which is characterized by temperance. (Temperance - moderation in all good things and abstinence from all harmful things). To live a full, rich and free life in Jesus Christ, membership in the WCTU requires abstinence from alcoholic beverages, tobacco products, illegal drugs and all other substances that would impair health and quality of life.*" Th e organization has also repeatedly campaigned zealously against the legalization of marijuana, demonstrating its firm stance for example in 1970, among other instances:

https://timesmachine.nytimes.com/timesmachine/1970/09/09/86396761.html and again in 2022: https://www.wctu.org/post/is-marijuana-medicine

[151] UN drug ban: Since 1971, the UN convention on psychotropic (psychoactive) substances has mandated that all signatory countries comply with its prohibition provisions: https://en.wikipedia.org/wiki/Convention_on_Psychotropic_Substances. The critical question is: to what extent can international agreements, once made, be relaxed or overturned when their harmful effects become evident? Despite over 100,000 drug-related deaths in the U.S. in 2021, there has been no significant shift in policy or change in public thinking. How many more lives must be lost before society wakes up? Is there some magic number that might trigger transition?

[152] Baum, Dan, 2016: https://harpers.org/archive/2016/04/legalize-it-all/. Richard Nixon's chief advisor, John Ehrlichman, later revealed that the war on drugs was also politically motivated. He admitted that its true purpose was to marginalize, suppress, and exclude two key groups: opponents of the Vietnam War and black communities.

[153] Methamphetamine: https://de.wikipedia.org/wiki/Methamphetamin. Marketed in Germany under the brand name *Pervitin*, was historically sold in various forms, including chocolates known as *Hausfrauenpralinen* (housewives' candy). These chocolates were promoted as an energy booster, particularly for housewives and workers, before the severe dangers of methamphetamine became widely recognized.

[154] Drug deaths – In the United States, drug-related deaths have surpassed 100,000 annually, with one person dying from an overdose every five minutes: **https://www.tagesschau.de/ausland/amerika/drogentote-US-101.html**. According to a recent report by the health authorities, this marks a tragic new record. In 2021, crystal meth alone was responsible for over 30,000 of these fatalities.

[155] Statistics on the global war on drugs: https://thehighcourt.co/war-on-drugs-statistics/

[156] See Tagesschau ibid.

[157] Personal communication Torsten Holmer.

[158] Legalization of drugs: https://en.wikipedia.org/wiki/Drug_liberalization. Despite the very detailed list outlining a wealth of various well-reasoned arguments for legalization, why does no one listen? Why do we demonize those who support it? Who truly benefits from the ongoing restrictions? The current prohibition empowers law enforcement agencies that demand ever-increasing resources including manpower to combat the rise in drug use. They help conservative politicians who exploit this issue to get re-elected with warnings about the danger of drugs. They benefit organized crime, for which the illegal drug trade remains a vast and ever-growing source of profit. De facto, the World Health Organization and the United States dictate this obviously dysfunctional strategy of repression, exacerbating social and economic hardship in the name of the war on drugs. Could it be that those who defend prohibition fear not just the consequences of legalization, but also the moral reckoning that would come with acknowledging decades of failed policies?

[159] Personal communication Torsten Holmer.

[160] Osbone, Diane K.: p. 16

[161] Tony Holbrook in his role as Chief Technical Officer of AMD Inc. https://www.ic-mrindia.org/free%20resources/casestudies/Business%20Strat-egy/AMD%20in%202005-Exhibits2.htm on January 18, 2024.

[162] Schwartz, Peter's *The Art of the Long View. Planning for the future in an uncertain world.* (Currency Doubleday, New York, 1991). Explores the principles of scenario planning from the author's own perspective. Schwartz, who led scenario planning at Shell for many years, later founded the consulting firm Global Business Network GBN in California. Today, GBN supports companies worldwide to navigate uncertainty through strategic foresight and long-term scenario planning.

Thank you for reading this book. I hope you enjoyed it.